Financial Fitness for Life®

Teacher Guide

Grades 6-8

Barbara Flowers
Sharon Laux
Authors, Second Edition

Barbara Flowers
Sheryl Szot Gallaher
Authors, First Edition

COUNCIL FOR
**Economic
Education**

Teaching Opportunity®

AUTHORS, SECOND EDITION:
Barbara Flowers
Senior Economic Education Specialist
Federal Reserve Bank of St. Louis

Sharon C. Laux
Associate Director
University of Missouri - St. Louis Center for Enterpreneurship and Economic Education

AUTHORS, FIRST EDITION:
Barbara Flowers
Senior Economic Education Specialist
Federal Reserve Bank of St. Louis

Sheryl Szot Gallaher
Director
Governors State University, Office of Economic Education

PROJECT DIRECTOR:
Richard A. MacDonald
Senior Advisor for Program Development
Council for Economic Education
and
Assistant Professor of Economics
St. Cloud State University

PROJECT COORDINATORS:
Christopher Caltabiano
Vice President for Program Administration
Council for Economic Education

Irina Piven
Senior Program Associate
Council for Economic Education

EDITOR:
Richard Western

DESIGN AND LAYOUT:
Jill O'Leske
Impact Design, LLC

Presented by:

This publication was made possible through funding by the Bank of America Charitable Foundation.

ISBN 1-56183-694-9   5 4 3 2 1

Acknowledgments

AUTHOR SUPPORT TEAM:

Becky Forristal, Seventh Grade Teacher
Rockwood Valley Middle School
St. Louis, MO

Joseph G. Maiden, Seventh Grade Teacher
Fox Middle School
Arnold, MO

Melanie Vierling, Grades 6-8
L'Ouverture Middle Academy
St. Louis, MO

Kristen A. Wimbley, Sixth Grade Teacher
McKinley Classical Leadership Academy
St. Louis, MO

CONTENT REVIEWERS:

Kris Bertelsen
St. Charles High School
St. Charles, MN

Nathan Eric Hampton
St. Cloud State University
St. Cloud, MN

Scott Wolla
Federal Reserve Bank of St. Louis
St. Louis, MO

Table of Contents

Foreword to the Second Edition

The Council for Economic Education (CEE) is proud to introduce the second edition of *Financial Fitness for Life*®. For ten years teachers have been using this resource to advance personal finance education among K-12 students across the nation. We now are pleased to bring an updated edition to a new generation of teachers, students, and parents.

The second edition retains the best of what the curriculum has always offered, with expertly written content and instructional plans for active learning. At the same time, we have made improvements that reflect a decade of teacher feedback. In addition to updating content, we have revised our teacher guides in an effort to make them more user-friendly. The new lessons follow CEE's standard structure and feature fewer graphic elements, making them easier to read and use.

We also have extended the educational resources provided on the companion website, http://fffl.councilforeconed.org/, where teachers can find supplementary lesson activities. The website also contains lesson correlations to state standards and downloadable visuals, among other features.

For over sixty years the CEE has envisioned a world in which people are empowered through economic and financial literacy to make informed and responsible choices throughout their lives as consumers, savers, investors, workers, citizens, and participants in our global economy. Given our dual missions of advocacy and education, we aim to ensure that sound economic decision-making skills are taught early, incrementally, and well throughout the K-12 curriculum.

The importance of our mission has become even more evident in the decade since *FFFL* was first published. According to the CEE's sixth *Survey of the States 2009: Economic, Personal Finance, and Entrepreneurship Education in Our Nation's Schools*, the number of states requiring students to take a personal finance course as a high school graduation requirement has increased dramatically, from one state in 1998 to 13 in 2009. Forty-four states now have content standards in personal finance education—up from 21 in 1998. With the increasing awareness of the importance of economic and financial education, there has never been a better time to reintroduce *FFFL*.

We would like to thank the Bank of America Charitable Foundation for its long-term and consistent support. The Bank believes that a strong foundation in financial literacy basics is a critical skill for future economic success. Bank of America wants to help create a generation of young people who can grow into adulthood with the know-how to use the financial system to earn, save, spend, budget, invest and manage credit. The Foundation's continued commitment to economic and financial education makes it a true leader and a positive example for others to follow. Their support and partnership have made *Financial Fitness for Life* possible.

Council for Economic Education

Foreword to the First Edition

For more than 50 years, the National Council on Economic Education (NCEE) has been calling attention to the need to educate our young people effectively in the skills of economics and personal finance and showing how that need can best be met. These new materials for teachers, sponsored by the Bank of America Foundation, provide an excellent and dramatic step in the direction of improving economic and financial literacy.

NCEE is proud of this splendid partnership with the Bank of America Foundation—and of the product.

We have found that students exposed to the economic way of thinking are more self-confident and more competent in making financial decisions, building their careers, and acting as informed citizens. By gaining understanding of the "real" world, we increase our prospects for better lives. Thanks to this distinctive program, we can now improve substantially on that kind of learning-for-life for millions of young people—who are our future.

NCEE's new multifaceted, comprehensive, and integrated program addresses the issue of economic and financial illiteracy by offering teaching-learning materials at four levels—grades K-2, 3-5, 6-8, and 9-12. There are 15 to 22 lessons in each part. Content for each of the grade levels is based on the Voluntary National Content Standards for Economics, which NCEE wrote and published, as well as the national guidelines for personal finance. Lessons are geared to active learning with games, simulations, role-playing, and computer use. All of the materials are also correlated with the extensive educational tools in personal finance and economics on our web site: www.ncee.net.

One exciting feature of these outstanding materials is that, for the first time, NCEE is offering parent guides for each educational level. Our research shows that students learn a considerable amount of their economic decision-making abilities from their parents. So NCEE is committed to assisting parents in the practical education of their children. These guidebooks are fun, as well as informative and instructive, for both students and their parents.

Nationally recognized experts in personal finance and economic education wrote the materials. Other experts and practitioners in the field reviewed them. The materials were then field-tested in three states over a period of two months. Each lesson was used by at least six teachers in urban, suburban, and rural settings. Refinements were made in the lessons according to the reviews from the field testing.

We are proud of the results—which will now become the leading edge of personal finance education for all students K-12.

Our thanks go to many people for this important development. Without the visionary philanthropy of the Bank of America Foundation, this project would not have been possible. We are also indebted to the authors of each set of documents; their dedication, insight, and creativity will become immediately apparent to users of these materials in the classroom and at home. We are grateful as well to the reviewers of the materials, and to the teachers, parents, and students in California, Florida, and Texas who field-tested the materials. Finally, and especially, we thank Dr. John E. Clow who directed the developmental work; because he has worked in the vineyard of economic and personal financial education for several decades, his knowledge of the field has been invaluable in orchestrating this significant project.

Council for Economic Education

Introduction

Financial Fitness for Life® (*FFFL*) provides high-quality instructional materials for use with students from kindergarten to grade 12. These materials are presented in separate publications for four grade levels (K-2, 3-5, 6-8, 9-12); within the grade levels, lessons are clustered in themes. The overarching goal of the materials is to help students make thoughtful, well-informed decisions about important aspects of personal finance, including earning income, spending, saving, borrowing, investing, and managing money.

The teacher and student guides are intended to work in tandem; the teacher guides contain the pedagogy and lesson descriptions while the student guides contain the corresponding exercises to be used in and out of the classroom.

All lessons are based on real-world concepts, and are presented in a manner that reinforces learning through practice. Features common to all grade levels include the following:

1. *FFFL* **materials are based on national standards.** A matrix at each of the four grade levels shows how lesson content correlates to standards in economics, personal finance, mathematics (K-8), and language arts (K-5).

2. *FFFL* **materials engage students in the economic way of thinking.** Concepts from economics provide the organizing framework and logic by which students learn how to make good decisions, and, equally important, how to avoid poor ones. The emphasis on economics concepts and the economic way of thinking distinguishes these materials from others used to develop personal financial literacy.

3. *FFFL* **materials call for active learning.** Lesson procedures describe engaging, hands-on instructional activity designed to reinforce students' understanding through applications and practice.

4. *FFFL* **materials address concepts in a developmentally appropriate manner.** Lessons for younger students frequently emphasize narrative, drama, and physical representations of economics and personal finance concepts. Lessons for older students illustrate certain uses of more abstract representations. The developmental approach to learning has been a hallmark of Council for Economic Education materials for several decades.

5. *FFFL* **materials emphasize a variety of teaching methods compatible with different learning styles.** Role playing, group discussions, gathering information from the Internet, reading materials, interviewing individuals, drawing pictures, and analyzing case studies are some of the many teaching methods found in the materials. Additional resources are available online at http://fffl.councilforeconed.org/.

6. *FFFL* **materials are reinforced by assessments.** Assessments are provided at the end of each theme.

7. *FFFL* **materials invite parents to play a role.** Parents can play an important role in developing their children's personal financial literacy. *FFFL* lessons for each level are accompanied by a parent guide. These guides provide background information and activities, linked to the lessons, which parents may use to reinforce and extend their children's understanding of topics in personal finance.

TABLE
1

Correlation of Lessons with National Standards in Mathematics*

⬇ Standards/Lessons ➡	1	2	3	4	5	6	7	8	9	10	11	12	13	14	15	16	17
NUMBER AND OPERATION																	
Understand numbers, ways of representing numbers, relationships among numbers and number systems.																	
Work flexibly with fractions, decimals, and percents to solve problems.			✓		✓	✓						✓	✓		✓		
Develop meaning for percents greater than 100 and less than 1.												✓					
Develop an understanding of large numbers and recognize and appropriately use exponential, scientific, and calculator notation.													✓				
Use factors, multiples, prime factorization, and relatively prime numbers to solve problems.													✓		✓		
Understand meanings of operations and how they relate to one another.																	
Understand the meaning and effects of arithmetic operations with fractions, decimals, and integers.			✓		✓	✓									✓		
Compute fluently and make reasonable estimates.																	
Select appropriate methods and tools for computing with fractions and decimals from among mental computation, estimation, calculators or computers, and paper and pencil, depending on the situation, and apply the selected methods.			✓		✓								✓				
Develop and analyze algorithms for computing with fractions, decimals, and integers and develop fluency in their use.													✓				

*Standards taken from Principles and Standards for School Mathematics, the National Council of Teachers of Mathematics (NCTM), 2000.

TABLE 1

Table 1 CONTINUED

Standards/Lessons	1	2	3	4	5	6	7	8	9	10	11	12	13	14	15	16	17
MEASUREMENT																	
Apply appropriate techniques, tools, and formulas to determine measurements.																	
Solve problems involving scale factors, using ratio and proportion.													✓		✓		
DATA ANALYSIS AND PROBABILITY																	
Develop and evaluate inferences and predictions that are based on data.																	
Use observations about differences between two or more samples to make conjectures about the populations from which the samples were taken.				✓													
PROBLEM SOLVING																	
Solve problems that arise in mathematics and in other contexts.							✓			✓			✓		✓		
COMMUNICATION																	
Communicate their mathematical thinking coherently and clearly to peers, teachers, and others.			✓														
CONNECTIONS																	
Recognize and apply mathematics in contexts outside of mathematics.		✓			✓	✓						✓		✓			
REPRESENTATION																	
Use representation to model and interpret physical, social, and mathematical phenomena.				✓													

Correlation of Lessons with National Standards in Economics*

▼Standards/Lessons▶	1	2	3	4	5	6	7	8	9	10	11	12	13	14	15	16	17
1. Scarcity	✓		✓	✓	✓	✓	✓			✓	✓		✓		✓		
2. Decision Making		✓					✓	✓			✓						✓
3. Allocation																	
4. Incentives			✓														
5. Trade																	
6. Specialization																	
7. Markets and Prices																	
8. Role of Prices											✓						
9. Competition and Market Structure																	
10. Institutions											✓		✓				
11. Money and Inflation														✓			
12. Interest Rates										✓	✓	✓	✓		✓		
13. Income				✓		✓											
14. Entrepreneurship					✓												
15. Economic Growth					✓	✓											
16. Role of Government and Market Failure									✓								
17. Government Failure																	
18. Economic Fluctuations																	
19. Unemployment and Inflation																	
20. Fiscal and Monetary Policy																	

*Standards taken from National Content Standards in Economics, 2nd ed., Council for Economic Education (CEE), 2010.

FINANCIAL FITNESS FOR LIFE: Teacher Guide Grades 6-8
http://fffl.councilforeconed.org/6-8

TABLE 2

TABLE 3

Correlation of Lessons with National Standards in Personal Finance*

⬇ Guidelines/Lessons ➡	1	2	3	4	5	6	7	8	9	10	11	12	13	14	15	16	17
FINANCIAL RESPONSIBILITY AND DECISION MAKING																	
Apply reliable information and systematic decision making to personal financial decisions																	
1. Take responsibility for personal financial decisions		✓	✓	✓	✓	✓	✓	✓		✓	✓	✓	✓	✓	✓		✓
2. Find and evaluate financial information from a variety of sources								✓						✓			✓
3. Summarize major consumer protection laws																	✓
4. Make financial decisions by systematically considering alternatives and consequences	✓	✓	✓	✓	✓		✓	✓		✓	✓	✓	✓	✓	✓		✓
5. Develop communication strategies for discussing financial issues							✓										✓
6. Control personal information								✓									
INCOME AND CAREERS																	
Use a career plan to develop personal income potential																	
1. Explore career options				✓	✓												
2. Identify sources of personal income					✓							✓					
3. Describe factors affecting take-home pay				✓	✓	✓			✓								
PLANNING AND MONEY MANAGEMENT																	
Organize and plan personal finances and use a budget to manage cash flow																	
1. Develop a plan for spending and saving		✓					✓		✓			✓					✓
2. Develop a system for keeping and using financial records								✓									
3. Describe how to use different payment methods								✓							✓		
4. Apply consumer skills to purchase decisions		✓	✓														✓
5. Consider charitable giving			✓														
6. Develop a personal financial plan							✓										
7. Examine the purpose and importance of a will																	

*Standards taken from National Standards in K-12 Personal Finance Education, Jump$tart Coalition for Personal Financial Literacy, 2007.

Table 3 CONTINUED

Guidelines/Lessons ➡	1	2	3	4	5	6	7	8	9	10	11	12	13	14	15	16	17
CREDIT AND DEBT																	
Maintain creditworthiness, borrow at favorable terms, and manage debt																	
1. Identify the costs and benefits of various types of credit															✓		
2. Explain the purpose of a credit record and identify borrowers' credit report rights																✓	
3. Describe ways to avoid or correct debt problems															✓	✓	
4. Summarize major consumer credit laws																	✓
RISK MANAGEMENT AND INSURANCE																	
Use appropriate and cost-effective risk management strategies																	
1. Identify common types of risks and basic risk management methods																	
2. Explain the purpose and importance of property and liability insurance protection																	
3. Explain the purpose and importance of health, disability, and life insurance protection																	
SAVING AND INVESTING																	
Implement a diversified investment strategy that is compatible with personal goals.																	
1. Discuss how saving contributes to financial well-being										✓	✓	✓	✓				
2. Explain how investing builds wealth and helps meet financial goals												✓	✓	✓			
3. Evaluate investment alternatives											✓	✓		✓			
4. Describe how to buy and sell investments														✓			
5. Explain how taxes affect the rate of return on investments																	
6. Investigate how agencies that regulate financial markets protect investors																	

FINANCIAL FITNESS FOR LIFE: Teacher Guide Grades 6-8
http://fffl.councilforeconed.org/6-8

Downloading Visuals, Activities, and Related Materials

On the Web

To download the visuals and activities for each lesson, find online lessons to extend the student activities and find related material to each lesson, visit:

http://fffl.councilforeconed.org/6-8

Resources Are Scarce

LESSON DESCRIPTION AND BACKGROUND

The students examine hypothetical companies that produce various goods made from wood. They discover that some companies do better than others at producing goods that people want to buy. The companies that produce goods that people want to buy at prices high enough for the producer to be profitable will be successful.

The lesson introduces students to concepts that help to describe and explain many important personal finance decisions. The concepts include productive resources, scarcity, and price. Resources are required to produce every good and service we want, but all resources are scarce and command a price. Thus, each good or service will also command a price. In our day-to-day lives, similarly, our resources are scarce. We can't have everything we want; in our personal finance decisions, therefore, we must try to satisfy our wants within the limits of budget constraints.

Lesson 1 correlates with national standards for mathematics and economics, and with personal finance guidelines, as shown in Tables 1-3 in the introductory section of this publication.

ECONOMIC AND PERSONAL FINANCE CONCEPTS

- Capital resources
- Human resources
- Natural resources
- Entrepreneur
- Scarcity
- Unlimited wants

OBJECTIVES

At the end of this lesson, the student will be able to:

- Define and provide examples of **natural resources**, **human resources**, **capital resources**, and **entrepreneur**.
- Explain that resources are scarce.
- Explain that resources are allocated by markets to provide the goods and services people want most.
- Explain that because resources are scarce, we must pay a price for using them.

TIME REQUIRED

Two 45-minute periods

MATERIALS

- A transparency of **Visual 1.1**, **1.2**, **1.3**, and **1.4**
- A copy for each student of **Introduction to Theme 1** and **Introduction** and **Vocabulary** sections of **Lesson 1** from the *Student Workbook*
- A copy of **Exercise 1.1** from the *Student Workbook*, with the company cards cut out so that each group of 4 or 5 students receives one of the cards.
- A copy of **Exercise 1.2** from the *Student Workbook*.
- Index cards

ADDITIONAL RESOURCES

To download visuals, find related lessons, correlations to state standards, interactives, and more, visit http://fffl.councilforeconed.org/6-8/lesson1.

PROCEDURE

1. Introduce the idea of unlimited wants by giving each student an index card. Ask the students to list on their cards all the things they want that can be bought with money (i.e., no listing of intangibles, such as world peace).

2. After three minutes, ask the students if they have listed everything they want. **(Most will probably say they have not.)**

3. Explain that human wants are unlimited. For most people, it is always possible to think of one more thing that it would be nice to have. Thus, even if the students had more than three minutes to write their lists, they would probably not be able to list all the things they want.

4. Tell the students to write down approximate prices next to each of the items on their lists. Then call on volunteers to give examples of items they listed and the prices they put down for those items. Briefly discuss the accuracy of the price listings. Ask: Could you afford to buy any of these items right now? **(Answers will vary; some students might be able to afford some of the items they have listed right now.)**

5. Tell the students to divide the price of each item by two. Ask: Could you afford to buy more of the items now, at this new price? **(The students most likely will say that they could afford to buy more items at the new price.)**

6. Tell the students to draw a line through each price they have listed, including the new half-off price, because now everything on the list is free. Ask: What additional items would you add to your lists if all items on the list were free?

7. Distribute a copy of **Introduction to Theme 1** and **Introduction** and **Vocabulary** sections of **Lesson 1** from the *Student Workbook* to each student. Have the students review the handouts and discuss them briefly, if necessary.

8. Explain that in the following portions of the lesson, the students will discover why the items on their lists are not free, and why some items are priced higher than others. The explanation will involve a consideration of "natural resources," "human resources," "capital resources," and the role of "entrepreneurs."

9. Begin with natural resources. Divide the class into groups of four or five students. Distribute a company card from **Exercise 1.1** from the *Student Workbook* to each group of students. Optional: You may wish to provide each student with their own copy of their comapny's card. Explain that you own a valuable resource, wood. You have only two units of wood available for sale. You will sell your wood at an auction, to the highest bidder. The bidders will be the companies that are represented by each group of students.

10. Begin an auction to sell your wood at $5 per unit; increase your asking price at $5 increments. Only two companies, Triple A Bat Company and Buckingham Furnishings, will be able to pay $30 per unit. After the auction, ask students from each group to read their company's story to the rest of the class.

11. Explain that wood is used in many ways, from building homes to making pencils. Companies that produce goods made from wood must buy from wood producers. However, there are only so many forests available for harvesting wood. Wood is scarce.

12. Explain that companies must produce goods that consumers are willing and able to buy at a price that is high enough for the producer to earn a profit and stay in business.

13. Ask the following questions.

   a. Why couldn't the Maple Wooden Hat Company buy wood to make more hats? **(Consumers were not willing to buy wooden hats. Wooden hats are uncomfortable and impractical.)**

   b. Why couldn't the Fanciful Furniture Company buy more wood to make more tables? **(Consumers were not willing to buy the colorful furniture.)**

   c. Why couldn't Premier Ashtray Company buy more wood to make more ashtrays? **(Consumers were not willing to buy** *ashtrays. The number of smokers in the country has been going down steadily over the past several years.)*

d. Why couldn't the Fold 'n Go Chair Company buy more wood to make more chairs? *(Consumers were not willing to buy the chairs. They were heavy and cumbersome.)*14. Explain that the price of goods made from wood reflects the price of wood. If there were a never-ending supply of trees, wood would be free, and products made from wood would be much less expensive.

14. Display **Visual 1.1**. Shield the visual from the students, revealing only the Natural Resources line. Define "natural resources" as resources that occur naturally in and on the earth; explain that natural resources are used to produce goods and services. Discuss the following three examples:

a. Oil is a natural resource. What is oil used to produce? *(Help the students identify various uses for oil—in producing, e.g., gasoline, fuel for home heating, machine lubrication, and plastic.)*

b. Lead is a natural resource. What is lead used to produce? *(Glass on television sets, car and truck batteries, solder, wheel weights, radiation shields, etc.)*

c. Water is a natural resource. What is water used to produce? *(Recreation, at pools and fountains; steel; lead; irrigation for crops; restaurant meals; carwashes, and many other goods and services.)*

15. Explain that because these resources (and all others) are scarce, producers must be willing to pay a price that will direct the resources to their products. In other words, producers receive the resource because they are willing and able to pay the market price for it.

16. Divide the class into five groups. Distribute a copy of **Exercise 1.2** from the *Student Workbook* to each student. Assign each group one of the resources listed. Allow five or ten

minutes for students to name as many uses as possible for their natural resource.

17. When time is up, ask students from each group to report their findings. As an optional activity, allow the students to add to their lists by researching uses on the Internet. Display **Visual 1.2** and ask the following questions.

a. What uses do we have for water? *(Answers might include swimming, drinking, bathing, flushing toilets, operating carwashes, cooking, irrigation, brushing teeth, making paper, creating electricity, cooling nuclear plants, etc.)*

b. Seventy percent of the earth is covered by water, but 97 percent of that water is in the oceans. Why is water scarce? *(We have a limited supply of fresh water, and many uses for it.)*

c. What uses do we have for oil? *(Answers might include producing gasoline, kerosene, jet fuel; lubricating engines and industrial machines; producing paint, detergent, asphalt, plastics, medicines, ink, the soles of sneakers, man-made fibers for clothing, curtains, and carpets.)*

d. There are approximately 1.3 trillion barrels of oil reserves in the world. The world consumes about 85 million barrels of oil each day. (Source: BP Statistical Review of World Energy 2008.) Some people estimate that we have a supply for roughly 40 years of oil use in known reserves. Why is oil scarce? *(We have a limited supply of oil, and many uses for it.)*

e. What uses do we have for one city block of land? *(Answers might include establishing a skate park, a dog park, a wading pool, a fountain; building houses, apartments, stores, a church, a school, a playground, a homeless shelter, a sculpture park, a community garden, a parking lot, etc.)*

f. What uses do we have for 10 city blocks of land? *(Answers might include building a business district, a zoo, a science center, a botanical garden, houses, an industrial park, a stadium, a museum district, a park, a high school, a cemetery, etc.)*

g. Why is land scarce? *(We have a limited supply of land, and many uses for it.)*

h. What uses do we have for sand? *(Answers might include producing bricks, asphalt, glass, concrete, plaster, sand boxes, sand paper; providing traction for tires; creating sand traps on golf courses; replenishing eroded beaches. Furthermore, any families that have built sandboxes know that they had to pay someone to acquire the sand—a sure sign that sand is a scarce resource.)*

i. We seem to have a lot of sand, but do we have enough? Why or why not? *(We do not have enough sand because we have so many uses for sand. If you made a long list of these uses, someone could always think of one more that you forgot.)*

18. Turn to human resources. Reveal the Human Resources line on **Visual 1.1** and define "human resources" as people performing mental or physical work to produce a good or service. Explain that human resources are also scarce; thus, there is a price for the services of human resources. When a producer of baseball bats pays for a worker, the money the worker earns increases the cost of producing bats. Thus somebody who buys a bat pays for the wood that goes into the bat and for the work done by the worker who makes the bat.

19. Turn to capital resources. Reveal the Capital Resources line on **Visual 1.1** and define "capital resources" as manmade goods that are produced for the purpose of producing other goods and services. Examples of capital resources include machines, buildings, and tools. Baseball bat producers must have machines, such as saws, lathes and sanders, to shape the bats they produce. They pay a price for the machines they use, and the cost of the machines adds to the cost of the bats. So someone who buys a bat pays for the wood in the

bat, the work of the worker who makes the bat, and the machine that helps the worker do his or her work.

20. Continue with entrepreneurial ability. Reveal the Entrepreneur line on **Visual 1.1** and define an "entrepreneur" as a person who takes the risks and gathers the resources to provide a new or improved good or service to the marketplace. Each of the companies bidding for wood was begun by an entrepreneur who had confidence in his or her idea and took the risk to produce a product.

21. Display **Visual 1.3**. Explain the term "scarcity": It refers to the fact that human wants are unlimited, but the resources available to satisfy those wants are limited. This point has been illustrated in the foregoing discussions of water, oil, land, labor, etc.

CLOSURE

1. Display **Visual 1.4**, shielding all points except the first one: Productive resources are limited. Tell the students that this point about limited resources is an important element of something called the economic way of thinking. As they become familiar with the economic way of thinking, they will become better able to evaluate their own decisions and those of others.

2. Reveal the second point on **Visual 1.4**: People cannot have everything they want. Explain that because productive resources are scarce, producers must pay for the resources they need to produce goods and services. Consumers pay for those resources when they buy a good or service. (Do not reveal the other points on the Visual. They will be revealed in the next two lessons.)

3. Explain that no one has enough income to buy all the goods and services he or she wants. Therefore, consumers must learn to make wise choices—deciding which goods or services it is most important to buy.

4. Use the following questions to review the lesson:

a. How would you define "natural resources"? **(The term refers to resources that occur naturally in and on the earth; these resources are used to make goods and services.)**

b. How would you define "human resources"? **(The term refers to people performing mental or physical work to produce a good or service.)**

c. How would you define "capital resources"? **(The term refers to manmade goods that are produced for the purpose of producing other goods and services.)**

d. How would you define "entrepreneur"? **(The term refers to a person who takes the risk and gathers the resources to provide a new or improved good or service to the marketplace.)**

e. Why can't we have everything we want? **(Our resources are scarce.)**

f. How do we determine who should be able to obtain scarce productive resources? **(The resources typically go to those who are willing and able to pay for them.)**

ASSESSMENT

1. Define natural resource. **(Resources that occur naturally in and on the earth that are used to make goods and services.)**

2. Name two natural resources that were not mentioned in the lesson. **(Iron ore, sun, natural gas.)**

3. Define capital resource. **(Man-made goods that are produced for the purpose of producing other goods and services.)**

4. Name two capital resources that were not mentioned in the lesson. **(Hammer, delivery truck, drill, computer.)**

5. Define human resource. **(People performing mental or physical work to produce a good or service.)**

6. Define entrepreneur. **(A person who takes**

the risk and gathers the resources to provide a new or improved good or service to the marketplace.)**

7. Challenge question:

Why aren't wooden chairs free? **(The chair manufacturer must buy wood. Wood is scarce and is, therefore, only available to those producers who can pay the price for the wood. Manufacturers must charge customers for the cost of the wood and the other resources used to produce chairs.)**

EXTENSION

Students have examined alternative uses for scarce natural resources. Human resources are also scarce. Students can examine why human resources are also scarce by looking at the alternative uses for human resources with similar skills. Refer students to http://www.payscale.com/best-colleges/popular-majors.asp to view different occupations students with various college degrees could choose.

Scarce Productive Resources

• **Natural Resources:** resources that occur naturally in and on the earth that are used to produce goods and services.

Examples: wood, oil, lead, water

• **Human Resources:** people performing mental or physical work to produce goods and services.

Examples: Doctors, teachers, trash haulers

• **Capital Resources:** manmade goods that are produced for the purpose of producing other goods and services.

Examples: Machines, computers, buildings, tools

• **Entrepreneur:** a person who takes the risk and gathers the resources to provide a new or improved good or service to the marketplace.

Example: Small-business owner

FINANCIAL FITNESS FOR LIFE: Teacher Guide Grades 6-8
http://fffl.councilforeconed.org/6-8

Scarce Natural Resources

Seventy percent of the Earth is covered by water, but 97 percent of that water is in the oceans. Of the remaining three percent of fresh water, much of it is in the form of glaciers.

• Why is water scarce?

There are approximately 1.3 trillion barrels of oil reserves in the world. The world consumes about 85 million barrels of oil each day. (Source: BP Statistical Review of World Energy 2008.) Some people estimate that we have a supply for roughly 40 years of oil use in known reserves.

• Why is oil scarce?

Scarcity

Wants > Resources = Scarcity

FINANCIAL FITNESS FOR LIFE: Teacher Guide Grades 6-8
http://fffl.councilforeconed.org/6-8

The Economic Way of Thinking

1. Productive resources are limited.

2. People cannot have everything they want.

3. People must make choices.

4. Every choice involves a cost.

5. People's choices have consequences.

6. People respond to incentives.

Making Decisions

LESSON DESCRIPTION AND BACKGROUND

This lesson builds on Lesson 1, introducing students to points 3 and 4 of The Economic Way of Thinking: People must make choices, and Every choice involves a cost. In activities related to these points, the students practice using the PACED decision-making process:

- State the **P**roblem.
- List **A**lternatives.
- Identify **C**riteria.
- **E**valuate alternatives based on criteria.
- Make a **D**ecision.

By explicitly identifying the alternatives and criteria for particular decisions, the students will gain skill in making decisions thoughtfully.

Lesson 2 is correlated with national standards for mathematics and economics, as well as national guidelines for personal financial management, as shown in Tables 1-3 in the introductory section of this publication.

ECONOMIC AND PERSONAL FINANCE CONCEPTS

- Alternatives
- Cost/benefit analysis
- Criteria
- Decision-making
- Opportunity cost
- Trade-offs

OBJECTIVES

At the end of this lesson, the student will be able to:

- Explain the purpose of a **decision-making** strategy
- Analyze a problem using the PACED **decision-making** process.

- Explain why some **criteria** are more important than others when using the **decision-making** process.
- Identify the **opportunity cost** of a decision.

TIME REQUIRED

Two 45-minute class periods

MATERIALS

- A transparency of **Visual 1.4** (from **Lesson 1**)
- A transparency of **Visual 2.1** and **2.2**
- A copy of the **Introduction** and **Vocabulary** sections from **Lesson 2** of the *Student Workbook* for each studet.
- A copy for each student **Exercise 2.1**, **2.2**, and **2.3** from the *Student Workbook*
- PACED grid sheet (available in **Visual 2.2** or in exercises from the *Student Workbook*)
- A copy of **Lesson 2 Assessment** from the *Student Workbook* for each student
- Product advertisements from newspapers or magazines
- 4" x 6" index cards (one per student)
- Construction paper and crayons or markers
- Three brands of graham crackers (or pretzels, soda crackers, etc.)
- Approximately 24 sandwich-sized plastic bags (Mark the bags A, B, and C. Place 4-5 crackers of one brand in each bag. Be sure to note which brand is A, which is B, and which is C.)
- Paper cups (one per student) and water.

ADDITIONAL RESOURCES

To download visuals, find related lessons, correlations to state standards, interactives, and more, visit http://fffl.councilforeconed.org/6-8/lesson2.

PROCEDURE

1. Introduce the lesson by telling the students you have noticed that people often make impulsive decisions about what to buy. Provide an example or two—perhaps people buying magazines or candy bars at the grocery store checkout counter. Explain that impulsive buying may not seem to be a big problem when the product in question is an 80-cent candy bar, but it certainly would not be a good idea to buy a big-ticket item—a $1,000 computer, say, or a $30,000 car—on impulse.

2. Assign the students to read the Introduction and Vocabulary sections for **Lesson 2** from the *Student Workbook*. Discuss the readings. Emphasize the importance of learning to make decisions thoughtfully, with careful attention to information related to each decision. Tell the students that if they begin to use sound decision-making strategies in minor situations, they will be better able to handle major decisions when they come along.

3. Tell the students that they will participate in a decision-making simulation. The purpose of the simulation is to demonstrate that good decisions are a result of identifying alternatives and evaluating those alternatives according to stated criteria.

4. Display **Visual 2.1**, The PACED Decision-Making Process, and review the five steps. Discuss the example on the visual, and ask the students to provide other examples of alternatives and criteria.

5. Emphasize the point that making a decision is the last step in the PACED process; the decision itself should come after identifying alternatives, identifying criteria, and evaluating alternatives against the criteria.

6. Introduce the graham-cracker-tasting activity. Tell the students that they will use a decision-making process to select their favorite graham cracker. (Other items could be used, such as pretzels, vanilla wafers, or soda crackers.) After they identify their criteria, they will test several crackers to decide which one meets their criteria for the best graham cracker.

7. Divide the class into groups of three or four students. Distribute a copy of **Exercise 2.1** from the *Student Workbook* to each student. Display **Visual 2.2**. Direct the students' attention to **Exercise 2.1**; tell the students to list (in the first row of the grid on **Exercise 2.1**) characteristics they would look for when choosing a graham cracker. These characteristics are called "criteria." *(The students will propose various criteria, probably including taste, color, aroma, crunchiness, price, and nutritional content. If the students choose price as a criterion, tell them that you will reveal the price of each cracker after the test. If they knew the prices before the test, price might influence their decision.)*

8. Show the students the bags of graham crackers. Point out the three brands: A, B and C. These are the "alternatives."

9. Distribute three bags of graham crackers (one bag each of brand A, B, and C) to each group; also distribute a small cup of water to each student.

10. Have the students taste the three different crackers. Instruct the students to "cleanse their palates" with some water between tastings of each alternative. Begin the evaluations with the criterion of taste. The alternative that best satisfies the taste criterion should receive a score of 3; the next-best alternative should receive a 2; and the third alternative should receive a 1. (These evaluations should be group decisions.)

11. Show the students how to complete the grid in **Visual 2.2**. Then have them continue to evaluate the crackers according to each of the other criteria, using the same "3-2-1" marking system. After they have assigned a number for each of the criteria in each of the alternatives, tell them

to sum up the rankings for each of the alternatives. The alternative with the highest total is the best choice for them.

12. When the groups have completed their evaluations and made their decision, discuss the simulation with the class, emphasizing again the importance of identifying criteria before evaluating alternatives and making a decision.

13. After each group has expressed its preference and stated its reasons, reveal the brands and the prices to the class, and allow time for discussion and reactions. Show prices both as price per box and unit price. Show the students how unit price is calculated by dividing the price of the box by the weight (in ounces, in this case). Often the students are surprised to find out that a less-expensive brand meets their criteria as well as, or better than, a higher-priced one.

14. Explain that some decisions, such as choosing the best graham cracker, are all-or-nothing decisions. (For example, if they were going to buy graham crackers, they would probably buy one brand and not another.) In an all-or-nothing situation, when a consumer chooses one alternative, she or he gives up another alternative. The next-best alternative given up is the "opportunity cost." (Suppose Brand A is Jane Doe's favorite cracker, followed by Brand C and Brand B; then, if she buys Brand A, Brand C is her opportunity cost—the next-best alternative.)

15. Introduce a new application of the PACED decision-making process, based on **Exercise 2.2** in the *Student Workbook*.

a. Distribute a copy of **Exercise 2.2** from the *Student Workbook* to each student and have them complete the exercise by working independently or in small groups.

b. Discuss the students' responses to the questions posed. *(Problem: At which store should I buy a new mp3 player? Alternatives: Party Time or Music Now. Criteria: large GB capacity, holds many songs, many hours of music playback, headphone jack, black finish, voice recorder. Evaluate: Answers will vary. Accept any reasonable explanations. Decision: Answers will vary. Opportunity cost: If they buy the mp3 player at one store, the mp3 player available at the other store is the opportunity cost. A completed decision-making grid is shown below.)*

c. Here again, explain that some choices, such as which mp3 player to buy, are likely to be all-or-nothing. If you buy an mp3 player at one store, you probably won't buy another mp3 player at another store. However, many choices involve "trade-offs"—i.e., giving up a little of one thing in order to get a little more of something else. Point out that if the students have ever studied for one hour instead of two, they have traded off one hour of studying for one hour of another activity, such as watching television.

16. Introduce the point that in some decisions, not all criteria are equally important. For a consumer buying a new music CD, for example, price may be important, but it may not be as important as the type of music. A loyal fan of a certain folk music group might choose to buy that group's latest release even if it costs more than a new release by a rap performer, or vice versa. Have the students suggest other examples of this point. *(Many possible responses: When buying a new bike, price may be more important than color. When choosing a hair stylist,*

Answers to Exercise 2.2

Criteria ➡ Alternatives ⬇	Large GB capacity	Holds many songs	Many hours of music playback	Headphone jack	Black finish	Voice recorder
Party Time	*no*	*no*	*no*	*yes*	*yes*	*no*
Music Now!	*yes*	*yes*	*yes*	*no*	*no*	*yes*

quality of work may be more important than price. When shopping for groceries, a wide selection of food products may be more important than a store's location, etc.)

17. Explain that when criteria have different degrees of importance, they can be given different values in the PACED grid. To develop this point, distribute a copy of **Exercise 2.3** from the *Student Workbook* to each student and have them read the opening paragraph.

18. Have the students complete **Exercise 2.3**, using the grid to record their answers. *(A completed grid for laptop computers is shown below: Row D is shaded; it shows the choice.)*

19. Discuss the second question posed after the grid in **Exercise 2.3**: Why should the Noga family buy the laptop computer you suggested? *(The students' explanations should include a discussion of how this particular product meets the Noga family's criteria better than other alternatives do.)*

CLOSURE

1. Display **Visual 1.4**, from **Lesson 1**. Reveal points 1 and 2 of the economic way of thinking and review them briefly, reminding the students

that resources are scarce, and therefore we cannot have everything we want. Then reveal point 3: People must make choices.

- Ask the students to list the choices they have made through the exercises in this lesson. *(They have made a choice about graham crackers, mp3 players, and computers.)*

- Review the steps used in the PACED decision-making model and point out that following those steps allowed them to make a careful decision.

2. Still using **Visual 1.4**, reveal point 4: Every choice involves a cost. Ask: What were the opportunity costs you experienced in making these decisions? *(The students' answers should reflect in each case the next-best alternative to the choice they made.)*

3. Distribute a 4" by 6" index card to each student. Also distribute construction paper and markers. Then display a number of advertisements from newspapers or magazines, pointing out the criteria stated or implied in each ad. *(e.g., An ad for a sports drink might mention taste, vitamin content, price, quick thirst-quenching, etc.).*

- Ask each student to write on his or her card a good or service he or she has purchased in

Answers to Exercise 2.3

Criteria ➡	Under $1,000	Minimum 15-inch screen	Minimum 2.5 hours battery run time	Green compliant	250 GB hard drive	Built-in camera	Total Value
Value **Alternatives**	5	4	3	4	4	2	
A	*5*	*0*	*0*	*4*	*0*	*0*	*9*
B	*5*	*4*	*0*	*0*	*4*	*2*	*15*
C	*5*	*4*	*3*	*0*	*0*	*0*	*12*
D	*5*	*4*	*3*	*4*	*4*	*2*	*22*
E	*5*	*0*	*0*	*0*	*0*	*0*	*5*
F	*5*	*0*	*3*	*4*	*4*	*0*	*16*

the past month. The students should also list the criteria that influenced them in the purchase of that product.

- Have the students exchange cards and use construction paper and markers to design an advertisement for the product on their cards, making sure to highlight and illustrate the criteria. (For example: If the item is a CD player, the advertisement might highlight criteria such as size, price, sound quality, number of functions, and portability.)

ASSESSMENT

Distribute **Lesson 2 Assessment**, Panel Discussion, from the *Student Workbook*. Divide the class into three groups - Groups A, B, and C. Allow time for the students to conduct research and prepare their panel discussions. *(Responses will vary; assess each group/ individual based upon the following: facts presented; relevance of facts to demographics of Group A, B, or C; appropriate use of the PACED decision-making process; clear, concise communication of information.)*

EXTENSION

Have the students look through their local newspapers for examples of decisions made by others. In particular, have them search for decisions that have been made regarding community goods and services (e.g., park or playground improvements, road repairs, new streetlights, etc.) Help students brainstorm alternative activities to those that were chosen and state what the criteria must have been in choosing the good or service.

The PACED Decision-Making Process

P State the **P**roblem.
A List **A**lternatives.
C Identify **C**riteria.
E **E**valuate alternatives based on criteria.
D Make a **D**ecision.

Problem: I don't have enough time to finish two big assignments.

Alternatives: I can do my math homework or finish my science project.

Criteria: I have an A average in math and a C average in science. The math assignment is worth 10% of my math grade; the science project is worth 35% of my science grade. I've missed two assignments in math; I haven't missed any assignments in science.

Evaluate: Because I'm not doing so well in science, and the science project is worth more, it's more important for me to finish the science project.

Decision: I'll finish the science project.

Which Graham Cracker Is Best?

Criteria → / ↓ Alternatives				Totals
A				
B				
C				

FINANCIAL FITNESS FOR LIFE: Teacher Guide Grades 6-8
http://fffl.councilforeconed.org/6-8

The Economic Way of Thinking

LESSON DESCRIPTION AND BACKGROUND

The students are introduced to the final two principles of the economic way of thinking.

- People's choices have consequences.
- People respond to incentives.

They engage in activities that require an analysis of choices, using the economic way of thinking.

Lesson 3 is correlated with national standards for mathematics and economics, and with personal finance guidelines, as shown in Tables 1-3 in the introductory section of this publication.

ECONOMIC AND PERSONAL FINANCE CONCEPTS

- Consequence
- Incentive
- Opportunity cost

OBJECTIVES

At the end of this lesson, the student will be able to:

- Identify the costs and benefits of a choice.
- Identify and evaluate **incentives**.
- Analyze choices and predict **consequences**.

TIME REQUIRED

Two 45-minute class periods

MATERIALS

- A transparency of **Visual 1.4** from **Lesson 1**
- A transparency of **Visual 3.1**, **3.2**, and **3.3**
- A copy of the **Introduction** and **Vocabulary** sections from **Lesson 3** of the *Student Workbook* for each student
- A copy for each student of **Exercise 3.1**, **3.2**, and **3.3** from the *Student Workbook*

- A copy for each student of **Lesson 3 Assessment** from the *Student Workbook*
- Calculators

ADDITIONAL RESOURCES

To download visuals, find related lessons, correlations to state standards, interactives, and more, visit http://fffl.councilforeconed.org/6-8/lesson3.

PROCEDURE

1. Open the lesson by having the students read the **Introduction** and **Vocabulary** sections for **Lesson 3**. Display **Visual 3.1**. By reference to the visual, introduce the lesson's focus on making choices. Explain that, in our everyday lives, we experience scarcity through our lack of time, space, and money. Time is limited: There are only 24 hours in each day to be used to accomplish everything we want to do. Space is limited: We have only so much land available for houses, schools, and shops. Money is limited: The things we want must be made from scarce "productive resources," which have a price. Because resources are scarce, we must make choices. No one earns enough money to have everything he or she wants. Ask the students to recall from **Lesson 1** the economic wants listed on the Bill and Melinda Gates Foundation website. *(**A clean and sanitary environment in areas of the world where people have no clean water and no sewerage system; eradication of diseases, such as HIV and malaria; public libraries with computers and Internet access; job training for young people; aid and support for victims of domestic violence.**)* Not even Bill Gates can have everything he wants!

2. Display **Visual 1.4** from **Lesson 1** and review the first four points. Read the first principle and discuss the following:

a. What are "natural resources"? *(Resources found in or on the earth; these resources are used to produce goods and services.)*

b. What are some examples of scarce natural resources? *(Many possible answers: Water, oil, coal, iron ore, etc. Choose one suggested answer to be used in c., below.)*

c. Name some goods and services that are produced using _____. *(Answers will vary depending on the natural resource chosen.)*

d. Can _____(name of natural resource) be used to make as many of these goods and services as we want? Why or why not? *(No. Students should recognize that there is no limit to the amount of these goods and services that we would want. They should state that there isn't a sufficient amount of this natural resource to make an unlimited supply of each good and service wanted.)*

3. Read the second principle of the economic way of thinking and ask the following questions:

a. What word do we use to describe this condition of having unlimited wants and limited resources? *(Scarcity.)*

b. Why can't people have everything they want? *(People's wants are unlimited, but productive resources are limited.)*

c. How do people solve the problem of unlimited wants and limited resources? *(People must make choices; they can't have everything they want.)*

4. Read the third principle of the economic way of thinking and ask the following questions:

a. There is a new movie out that everyone says must be seen on a large screen. On the other hand, there is a Monster Truck show in town this weekend. You have $10 and no time to earn any more money. Admission to each of these events is $10. You choose to go to one event. What economic term would you use to describe the event you did not choose? *(Opportunity cost.)*

b. Let's say these two events are your favorite choices. Then you find out that the circus is in town for the weekend. While trying to decide, you write the three events in your order of preference, 1. Monster Truck show, 2. movie, and 3. circus. Which of these events is your opportunity cost? *(The movie, because it is the next-best alternative you did not choose.)*

5. Reiterate that every choice involves an "opportunity cost": the next-best alternative that is given up when a choice is made. Display **Visual 3.2** and review the statements about how people have to make choices because scarce resources limit our time, space, and money.

6. Discuss **Visual 3.2**. Ask: What are the choices and opportunity costs in the three examples it poses? *(When Sofia chooses to study, her opportunity cost is not getting to read. When Maurice chooses to use his limited locker space for books, his opportunity cost is the space that could have been used for shoes. When Nguyen chooses to use his limited money to buy snacks, his opportunity cost is the movie ticket he could have bought.)*

7. Have the students suggest personal experiences that have involved limited time, space, or money. Have them identify their choices and opportunity costs in these experiences. *(The students should focus on their choices and what they had to give up in each instance. They should use the term "opportunity cost" as they discuss their choices and what they gave up.)*

8. Divide the class into pairs. Distribute a copy of **Exercise 3.1** from the *Student Workbook* to each student. Have the students complete the exercise, following the examples given in **Visual 3.2**. When the students have completed the exercise, engage them in a discussion of the statements they made. *(Sample answers: Shaundra can choose to get her mom a less-expensive gift, or she can tell her mom she'll have the gift for her later, after she saves more*

money. If she chooses the less-expensive gift, her opportunity cost is that she had to give up dollars that could have been used to make partial payment for the necklace. Angelo's alternatives are to keep an aquarium or a flat screen TV in his room. If he chooses the aquarium, his opportunity cost is the flat screen TV. Raul's alternatives are to take the time to raise $15 or to spend the time doing something else. If Raul chooses to spend his time doing something else, his opportunity cost is to participate in the raffle.)

9. Define "incentives" as factors that motivate and influence human behavior. Explain that incentives can come in the form of money or in other forms. "Monetary incentives" include money, income, and economic wealth. "Non-monetary incentives" motivate people for reasons other than money, wealth, or income. For example, parents might turn down higher-paying jobs in another town so that their children do not have to switch schools. Or a student might give up a baby-sitting job in order to spend time with friends.

10. Explain that in a market economy, self-interest is an important motivator, whether that interest is monetary or non-monetary. For example, "entrepreneurs" take risks in order to

start businesses, many of them hoping to make lots of money. However, they may also have non-monetary incentives, such as being their own boss or proving that they have good ideas.

11. Explain that non-monetary incentives can be physical, emotional, spiritual, or social. For example, people exercise to maintain good health and to look better. People in religious orders provide care and shelter for the poor and sick because of a spiritual incentive to help others.

12. Display **Visual 3.3**. Have the students suggest incentives that might help to explain the choices listed in the chart. **(Answers will vary; possible responses follow.)**

13. Again, divide the class into pairs of students. Explain that when consumers are presented with different economic choices, they must consider both the benefits (what you gain) and the costs (what you give up) of each choice to determine which one offers the greatest economic incentive.

14. Distribute a copy of **Exercise 3.2** from the *Student Workbook* to each student; also distribute calculators. Have the students calculate the savings they would enjoy from each coupon; determine which is the better incentive in each instance; and record their decision and an explanation on the answer sheet. **(Answers are on the following page.)**

Answers to Visual 3.3

Choices	Monetary Incentives	Non-monetary Incentives
Save half of earned babysitting money in a savings account	Parents agree to match your savings, dollar for dollar	**You want to make a donation of money to the local food pantry (spiritual, emotional, or social)**
Buy a new bike	**Price of bike is reduced**	You can get exercise by riding the bike (physical)
Lend $10 to a classmate	**Your friend agrees to pay you $11 at the end of the month for a $10 loan today**	**The classmate is a good friend (emotional or social)**
Join a walk-a-thon for charity	**Every participant gets a free T-shirt (although this may be considered a non-monetary incentive)**	**You feel good about yourself when you help others (spiritual or emotional)**

15. Distribute a copy of **Exercise 3.3** from the *Student Workbook* to each student. Have the students work in small groups to complete the exercise. Discuss their answers. *(1. Finances were limited; the students did not have enough money to pay for both a DJ and a video-sound show. 2. The committee chose the video-sound show. 3. Its incentive was the expectation of making more money and achieving higher attendance. 4. The opportunity cost of choosing the video-sound show was the choice of having the DJ. 5. Cost: higher-priced entertainment carried risk of losing money. They also had to forgo the use*

of a DJ. Benefit: possibility of making more money because more students would attend. 6. Consequences were that a larger number of students attended the dance, and the Honor Society made more money than expected. They also took more risk as a consequence of their choice.)

CLOSURE

Display **Visual 1.4** and discuss the final two points. Explain to the students that the economic way of thinking involves understanding these six points. Have the students look through

Answers to Exercise 3.3

1. Incentive #1 is the better deal. **#1: 20% off = $29.99-$6.00 = $23.99** **#2: Save $5.00 = $29.99-$5.00 = $24.99**	**2. Incentive #2 in the better deal.** **#1: Two boxes cost $5.98, get one free. Therefore, 3 boxes cost $5.98, or $1.99 each ($5.98/3).** **#2: Save $1.50 on each box = $2.99-$1.50 = $1.49 each. Therefore, 3 boxes cost $4.47.**
3. Incentive #1 is the better deal. **#1: Two 32-oz. jars cost $2.56, or $1.28 each, or $0.04 per ounce.** **#2: Two 48-oz. jars cost $5.98, minus $.50 each = $4.98, divided by 96 ounces = $0.05 per ounce.**	**4. Incentive #2 is the better deal.** **#1: $69.95 + $34.98 = $104.93 for 2 pairs.** **#2: $100.00 for two pairs.**
5. Incentive #2 is the better deal. **#1: $5 off = $240 ($40 x 6 tickets) + $9.99 for root beer = $249.99.** **#2: $45 x 5 tickets = $225**	**6. Both incentives are the same.** **#1: 4 nights x $8.00 = $32.00; 2 nights x $4.00 = $8.00; $32 + $8 = $40** **#2: 5 nights x $8.00 = $40.00; 1 night free; total $40**
7. Incentive #1 is the better deal. **#1: $16.99 + $16.99 = $33.98** **#2: Two pizzas for $35.00**	**8. Incentive #2 is the better deal.** **#1: $35.99 + $35.99 + $49.99=$121.97 for three games** **#2: 3 games x $49.99 = $149.97 minus $29.99 (20%) = $119.98 for 3 games**

local newspapers to find articles about economic decisions. (Examples can be frivolous or serious, and can represent decisions in politics, entertainment, media, sports, business, etc.) Divide the class into groups and have each group analyze one decision, using principles from the economic way of thinking. Remind the students to examine choices, costs, benefits, incentives, and consequences. After the groups finish their analyses, engage the class in a discussion of each group's news articles and their analyses of the respective decisions.

ASSESSMENT

Distribute **Lesson 3 Assessment**, The Economic Way of Thinking, from the *Student Workbook*. Sample answers can be found in **Visual 3.4**.

EXTENSION

Have the students keep a diary of their economic and financial decisions for a week. After they complete the diary, have them write a description of one of the decisions, stating the incentives for choosing as they did and the opportunity cost and consequences associated with their choice.

Why Must We Choose?

Limited time, space, and money	+	Unlimited wants	=	People cannot have everything they want

Every Choice Has an Opportunity Cost

Because resources are scarce, people can't have everything they want; they have to make choices. Every choice involves an opportunity cost—the next-best alternative not chosen.

Because time is limited, people have to make choices.
- Example: Sofia must decide whether to finish her math assignment or read a book right after dinner. If she chooses to use her limited time to do the math assignment, the opportunity cost is reading the book.

Because space is limited, people have to make choices.
- Example: Maurice must decide whether to put books or gym shoes on the shelf in his locker. If he chooses to use the shelf space for books, the opportunity cost is space for his shoes.

Because money is limited, people have to make choices.
- Example: Nguyen must decide whether to spend his allowance for snacks or a movie ticket. If he chooses to buy snacks, the opportunity cost is the movie ticket.

Incentives Matter

Choices	Monetary Incentives	Non-monetary Incentives
Save half of earned babysitting money in a savings account	*Parents agree to match your savings, dollar for dollar*	
Buy a new bike		*You can get exercise by riding the bike (physical)*
Lend $10 to a classmate		
Join a walk-a-thon for charity		

FINANCIAL FITNESS FOR LIFE: Teacher Guide Grades 6-8
http://fffl.councilforeconed.org/6-8

Lesson 3 Assessment:
Answer Key

A. Examine the decisions made by the people in the following situations by using the economic way of thinking. Answers may vary. Some possible answers include:

1. Instead of putting an extra $3,000 in their retirement fund, Florence and Joe decided to fly from Chicago to Florida for a week of golf and relaxation.

Choice: *(Fly to Florida.)*

Opportunity Cost: *(Add $3,000 to their retirement fund.)*

Incentive: *(Chance to play golf and relax.)*

Consequences of their choice: *(Won a tournament; lost a golf club.)*

Benefits: *(Met new friends at the tournament; had a relaxing vacation.)*

2. Brian and Sheryl paid their credit card debt instead of making a down payment on a new convertible.

Choice: *(Paid credit card balance.)*

Opportunity Cost: *(Enjoyment of new convertible.)*

Incentive: *(Eliminate monthly payments and high interest charges.)*

Consequences of their choice: *(Had more money to save or spend on other purchases.)*

How did Brian and Sheryl benefit from their choice? *(Had more disposable income to spend or save because they no longer had to make monthly credit card payments.)*

3. Su-Zee, Lorena, and their friends went to the beach instead of working at the school book sale last weekend.

Choice: *(Weekend at the beach.)*

Opportunity cost: *(Spending time with other friends at the book sale.)*

Incentive: *(Get a suntan; enjoy time at the beach.)*

Consequences of their choice: *(Sunburn; friends at book sale angry that Su-Zee, Lorena, and friends didn't help at the book sale.)*

How did Su-Zee, Lorena, and their friends benefit from their choice? *(Nice tan, day of fresh air and exercise, fun at the beach.)*

B. Using the economic way of thinking, answer this question: Why do math teachers give homework every day?

Teacher's Choice: *(Give homework, have to check it.)*

Opportunity Cost: *(Free time with no homework to check.)*

Incentives for Making the Choice: *(Students will learn more; students will do better on tests.)*

Consequences of Choice: *(Missing good TV shows; less time with family.)*

Who benefits? How?: *(Students learn more, teachers get good evaluations from parents and adminstrators, teacher has a feeling of accomplishment.)*

Why Stay in School?

LESSON DESCRIPTION AND BACKGROUND

Against a background of information about the relationship between educational attainment, employment, and income levels, the students weigh decisions about education in light of costs and benefits.

Lesson 4 is correlated with national standards for mathematics and economics, and with personal finance guidelines, as shown in Tables 1-3 in the introductory section of this publication.

ECONOMIC AND PERSONAL FINANCE CONCEPTS

- Benefits
- Costs
- Income
- Marginal benefit
- Opportunity cost
- Wage

OBJECTIVES

At the end of this lesson, the student will be able to:

- Explain the **benefits** associated with levels of educational attainment.
- Explain the **costs** associated with levels of educational attainment.
- Define **opportunity cost**, and explain the **opportunity cost** of dropping out of school.

TIME REQUIRED

One 45-minute classroom session

MATERIALS

- A transparency of **Visual 4.1, 4.2,** and **4.3**
- A copy for each student of **Introduction to Theme 2** and **Introduction** and **Vocabulary** sections of **Lesson 4** from the *Student Workbook*
- A copy for each student of **Exercise 4.1** and **4.2** from the *Student Workbook*
- Calculators (one per student)
- Rulers (one per student)
- Unlined paper (one sheet per student)

ADDITIONAL RESOURCES

To download visuals, find related lessons, correlations to state standards, interactives, and more, visit http://fffl.councilforeconed.org/6-8/lesson4.

PROCEDURE

1. Begin by asking the students to draw a picture of a set of stairs, with at least five steps, from a side view. They should use only a pencil and unlined paper—no ruler or other guide. When they have completed their drawings, tell them to use their rulers to measure the vertical distance between each step by measuring the riser for each step. Have them write the measurement of each step by the riser. Ask: How many of you drew a set of stairs where the riser measurements were the same for each step? (Emphasize the number of students who have unequal risers.)

2. Ask all the students who think of school as an uphill climb to raise their hands. Explain that becoming educated is like climbing a set of stairs. However, the stairs the students climb to get an education are more like the stairs the students drew than the perfectly measured stairs we climb in our homes or in school. Some subjects in school and some levels of schooling take more effort; they require that we take bigger steps to reach the goal.

3. Distribute a copy of **Introduction to Theme 2** and **Introduction** and **Vocabulary** sections of **Lesson 4** from the *Student Workbook* to each student. Have the students review the handouts and discuss them briefly, if necessary. Then distribute a copy of **Exercise 4.1** to each student. Tell the students that they will conduct a brief self-inventory of the challenges they face in school. Direct their attention to the columns headed Difficult, Comfortable, and Easy on **Exercise 4.1**. Under the column headings, the students should list subjects, assignments, or skills related to their schoolwork that strike them as difficult, comfortable, or easy. For instance, some students might find math difficult, or might find some area of math, such as word problems, difficult. They might find writing easy but the oral presentation of their writing difficult. They might have difficulty with personal traits, such as study skills. They might find neatness and organization easy to master. As necessary, help the students get started with this task. (Retain the completed inventory sheets for the assessment and for parent involvement.)

4. Explain that just as certain subject areas and tasks may be difficult, comfortable, or easy, different levels of education may also be more difficult than others. However, each level brings rewards.

5. Have the students take home their completed self-inventories to show their parents. Ask the students to work with their parents to develop a plan for dealing with aspects of school work that seem difficult.

6. Display **Visual 4.1**. Explain that the set of stairs depicted on this visual represents different levels of educational attainment and the median income associated with each level. Note that the median level of income increases with each step, as educational attainment increases.

7. Distribute a copy of **Exercise 4.2** from the *Student Workbook* to each student. Ask the students to complete Question 1, calculating the differences in median income for a-d. *(a. $8,580; b. $7,540; c. $12,584; and d. $13,000)*. Point out that each difference is an

annual difference. For instance, someone with a bachelor's degree earns, on average, $12,584 more every year than the person with an associate's degree.

8. Note that the median level of income for a high school dropout is $22,152. Point out that this doesn't mean that someone who drops out of school at age 16 will earn $22,152. The "median wage" (for all working people without a high school diploma) means that half of those people earn more than this amount and half earn less than this amount.

9. Explain that at a certain age, depending on state laws, students can choose to get off the steps. They can simply stop after completing, say, the tenth grade, and move into the labor force. Or they can continue, step by step, to reach some other goal. Each step represents a benefit as well as a cost.

10. Define "marginal benefit" as the additional benefit that would be obtained from one more unit of some good or service. In the case of education, the marginal benefit could be the additional income per year that would result from one more year of education. The marginal benefit of education also includes the attainment of additional skills that could help people meet important challenges or gain additional job satisfaction. Point out that the marginal benefits would accrue for every year of a person's working life.

11. Refer the students back to **Exercise 4.2**. Have them calculate the lifetime earnings at each level of educational attainment (Question 2). Answers are given in the table on the next page.

12. Ask the students to focus their attention on someone who has dropped out of high school after tenth grade, and on someone who has graduated from high school. Assuming a working life of 52 years for the high school graduate and 54 years for the dropout, the students can find that the dropout's lifetime earnings will be $1,196,208 (54 x 22,152), while the high school graduate's lifetime earnings will be $1,598,064 (52 x 30,732). Ask: What is the lifetime difference in earnings? *($401,856)* Explain that one cost of dropping out

Answers to Exercise 4.2

	HS dropout	HS diploma	Associate's degree	Bachelor's degree	Master's degree
Annual income	$22,152	$30,732	$38,272	$50,856	$63,856
Years worked	54	52	50	48	46
Life earnings	$1,196,208	$1,598,064	$1,913,600	$2,441,088	$2,937,376

of school is the lifetime difference in earnings—in this case, $401,856, or approximately 25 percent lower earnings (401,856/1,598,064) for the high school dropout.

13. Explain an even more distressing point about high school dropouts: They are much more likely to be unemployed. Display **Visual 4.2**. Explain that the numbers shown represent United States average unemployment rates for 2008, by educational attainment. Ask the students to note the unemployment rate for people who attended only one-to-three years of high school **(9.0%)** and to compare that figure with the unemployment rate for high school graduates **(5.7%)**. Ask the students to speculate: Why would the unemployment rate be so much higher for those who have not completed high school? **(Those who dropped out probably have fewer skills and less knowledge, and are thus less valuable to employers.)** Prompt the students by asking what an employer's impression of a high school dropout might be.

14. Display **Visual 4.3**. Ask the students if these are fair assessments on the employer's part. **(The students will probably say that these assessments are unfair.)** Allow discussion, but explain that employers often have little information to go on when they are hiring someone. So they use certain measures, such as educational attainment, to determine who is likely to be a good employee. If a high school graduate and a high school dropout apply for the same job, and if their other attributes, such as skills or work experience, are approximately equal, it is almost a certainty that the high school graduate will get

the job.

15. Explain that the class has examined the benefits of staying in school, but they should know that there are also costs. What might those costs be? Ask:

a. What full-time jobs might be available to someone who is 17 years old? **(Retail clerk, fast food worker, car wash worker, etc.)**

b. What is the average hourly wage paid to people starting in those positions? **(Answers will vary, but the students should recognize that wage rates for these jobs vary from minimum wage to about $9.00 per hour.)**

c. Explain that at 40 hours per week, and 52 weeks per year, it is possible to work 2,080 hours per year. Tell the students to use the most optimistic point of this wage range, $9.00 per hour, and calculate the annual income for a worker earning that rate of pay. **(2,080 x 9 = $18,720)**

d. By reference to the above calculation, explain that people use money and time to obtain additional education. Allocating money and time to education involves opportunity cost. (As necessary, review the definition of "opportunity cost" as the next-best alternative given up when a decision is made.) The year's salary is the opportunity cost, or income not earned, for a person who attends school full-time for the year.

e. To pursue the analysis, tell the students to assume the same wage for a second year, and ask what the opportunity cost of finishing high school is **($18,720 + $18,720 = $37,440)**. Remind the students that a high school graduate will earn an average of

$401,856 more than a dropout over a lifetime, and will work two fewer years. Ask: Do the costs of completing high school outweigh the benefits, or do the benefits outweigh the costs? *(The benefits certainly outweigh the costs.)*

f. Explain that as students move on to college, the costs become significantly higher. Annual college tuition costs can range from an average of approximately $6,600 at a public university to an average of approximately $25,000 at a private university. These figures do not include housing costs, because such costs occur whether the student is in school or not. Ask: Are there are any other costs that must be considered when calculating the cost of attending college as a full-time student? *(The amount of forgone income that could otherwise be earned, fees, books, and supplies.)*

16. Refer the students again to **Visual 4.1**. Explain that as people increase their educational attainment they also increase their income. Ask: Why might the additional income be important? *(Answers will vary. Guide the students to recognize that greater incomes provide people with a wider range of choices about goods and services, and with greater financial security.)* Explain that higher educational attainment, in general, brings about greater income, which brings about a higher standard of living. Also, higher levels of educational attainment can bring about greater job satisfaction. People who have reached high levels of education generally have more choices about jobs.

CLOSURE

Use the following questions to review the lesson:

- At what level of educational attainment is there likely to be the greatest level of unemployment? *(The level of the high school dropout.)*

- Why is the unemployment rate so much higher for high school dropouts? *(Answers will vary. The students should recognize that the high school dropout is likely to*

be unskilled and that employers are less likely to believe a high school dropout can face the challenges of holding a job.)

- What are the benefits associated with increasing educational attainment? *(Greater incomes, higher standards of living, greater job satisfaction, more choices.)*

- As people consider the benefits of increasing their educational attainment, what must they also consider? *(The costs.)*

- What is opportunity cost? *(The next-best alternative given up when a choice is made.)*

- What is the opportunity cost of staying in high school until graduation? *(The wages that could have been earned during that period.)*

- In addition to forgone wages, what are some additional costs of attending college? *(Costs of tuition, fees, books, and supplies.)*

ASSESSMENT

Refer again to **Exercise 4.1** in the *Student Workbook* and the inventories the students conducted early in the lesson. Explain that the students' lists in the Easy column probably refer to their special aptitudes and skills. Ask each student to write a list of occupations that require the aptitudes and skills she or he listed in the Easy column. Then tell the students to choose one of those occupations and write a brief essay about it, including the following:

- The level of education required for this occupation,

- The costs of obtaining the education required in terms of time spent and lost earnings,

- The expected benefits in terms of financial rewards and fulfillment.

For help with their essays, the students can consult the *Occupational Outlook Handbook* at http://stats.bls.gov/oco/. They may also discover helpful information by interviewing someone in the occupation they are considering.

EXTENSION

Have the students interview an adult about his or her job, concentrating on the skills necessary in the job. Some questions might include:

- How did you acquire the skills necessary for your work?

- What were your academic strengths in school?

- How did school prepare you for the position you hold?

- What is your highest level of educational attainment?

FINANCIAL FITNESS FOR LIFE: Teacher Guide Grades 6-8
http://fffl.councilforeconed.org/6-8

Steps to Success

2009 Median Annual Earnings by Levels of Educational Attainment:

$65,364	Master's Degree
$53,300	Bachelor's Degree
$39,572	Associate's Degree
$32,552	High School Graduate
$23,608	Less Than High School

Source: Bureau of Labor Statistics, Current Population Survey, http://www.bls.gov/emp/emptab7.htm

Uneducated = Unemployed

Unemployment Rates
by Levels of Educational Attainment:

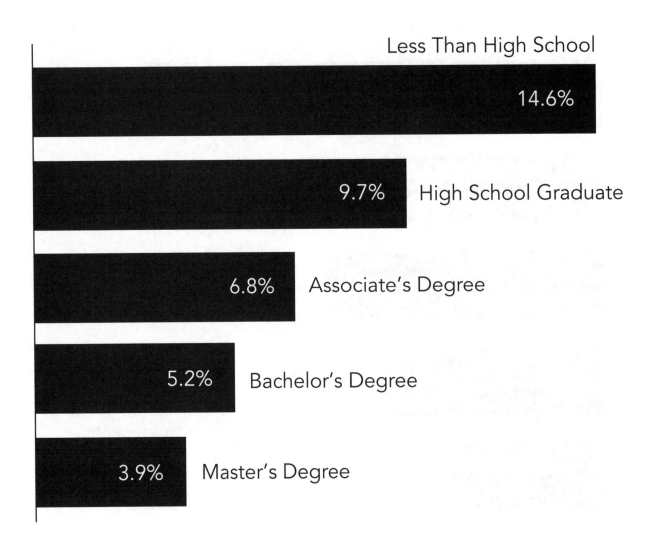

Less Than High School

14.6%

9.7% High School Graduate

6.8% Associate's Degree

5.2% Bachelor's Degree

3.9% Master's Degree

Note: Data are 2009 annual averages for persons age 25 and over.

Source: Bureau of Labor Statistics, Current Population Survey, http://www.bls.gov/emp/edupay.txt

FINANCIAL FITNESS FOR LIFE: Teacher Guide Grades 6-8
http://fffl.councilforeconed.org/6-8

An Employer's Perspective

"Someone who couldn't complete high school probably finds it difficult to complete any task."

"How bright can a high school dropout be?"

"High school can be hard work. A high school dropout is probably scared of a little hard work."

"A high school dropout didn't learn some things that are needed to perform well in this job."

Choosing a Career

LESSON DESCRIPTION AND BACKGROUND

The lesson focuses on a deliberate approach to making career choices. The students examine statistics projecting future demand for workers in various occupations. They complete a self-assessment to identify career pathways that match their interests and abilities. After examining a number of job descriptions, they compare each job's requirements to the skills recommended by SCANS (Secretary's Commission on Achieving Necessary Skills). Finally, they consider entrepreneurship as a career option.

People sometimes find their way into particular careers by haphazard means, influenced by chance occurrence and unreliable information. To make more deliberate, well-informed choices, young people need to understand the job market, identify their own aptitudes, and grasp the relationship between marketable skills and workplace success.

Lesson 5 is correlated with national standards for mathematics and economics, and with personal finance guidelines, as shown in Tables 1-3 in the introductory section of this publication.

ECONOMIC AND PERSONAL FINANCE CONCEPTS

- Entrepreneur
- Human capital
- Opportunity cost
- Productivity

OBJECTIVES

At the end of this lesson, the student will be able to:

- Assess his or her career interests in light of projected demand for workers in various occupations.
- Explain the relationship of **human capital** to career choices and opportunities.

- Recognize the importance of investment in **human capital**.
- Explain the relationship of worker **productivity** to education and experience.
- Describe the characteristics of an **entrepreneur**.
- Explain how **entrepreneurs** benefit the economy.

TIME REQUIRED

Two 45-minute class periods

MATERIALS

- A transparency of **Visual 5.1**, **5.2**, **5.3**, **5.4**, and **5.5**

- A copy for each student of the **Introduction** and **Vocabulary** sections from **Lesson 5** from the *Student Workbook*

- Copies of **Activity 5.1A** (enough for half of the class) and **5.1B** (enough for half of the class)

- Optional: Copies of **Activity 5.2A** (enough for half of the class) and **5.2B** (enough for half of the class)

- A copy for each student of **Exercise 5.1**, **5.2**, **5.3**, and **5.4** from the *Student Workbook*

- A copy for each student of **Lesson 5 Assessment** from the *Student Workbook*

- A stopwatch (or clock with a second hand)

- Poster board for each student

ADDITIONAL RESOURCES

To download visuals, find related lessons, correlations to state standards, interactives, and more, visit http://fffl.councilforeconed.org/6-8/lesson5.

PROCEDURE

1. Introduce the lesson's focus on career choices. Assign the students to read the **Introduction** and **Vocabulary** sections from the *Student Workbook* for **Lesson 5.** Explain that people considering any given career must take account of the knowledge, skills, and experience needed to work successfully in that career. Turn to an example. Ask: What knowledge, skills, and experience does the cook in the school cafeteria need to have? *(Knowledge of food safety requirements, reading and math skills to follow recipes and calculate measurements, experience using kitchen equipment, etc.)* Tell the students that the knowledge, skills, and experience in question are called the cook's "human capital."

2. Display **Visual 5.1**. Ask: What sort of human capital is needed by people working in these occupations? *(Answers will vary by occupation. Some suggested responses include: Pilot— Good vision and hand-eye coordination; knowledge of plane operation; understanding of weather patterns and air pressure; confidence. Marine Biologist—Unafraid of the water; education in biology and oceanography; apprenticeship in marine biology program; patience. Web Designer—Keyboarding; installing software; education in information technology; internship at a software company; creativity. TV Reporter—Pleasant voice; good reader; understanding and interest in geography, history and world events; college TV station or radio station experience; articulate.)*

3. Explain that the class will participate in a simulation activity called "Insiders and Outsiders" to learn more about "knowledge" as a component of human capital.

a. Divide the class into two teams: Group A and Group B.

b. Distribute a copy of **Activity 5.1A**, face down, to each student in Group A; distribute a copy of **Activity 5.1B**, face down, to each student in Group B.

c. Explain that this activity will be a timed exercise. The students are not to begin until they

are told to do so. When they complete the exercise, they should raise their hands, and you will call out their times. They should write their own times at the bottom of their activity sheet.

d. Explain that if any students have not completed the exercise at the end of five minutes, time will be called. Those students will receive a maximum score of five minutes.

e. Students who finish in fewer than five minutes should sit quietly and not disturb others who are attempting to complete the exercise.

4. To begin, instruct only the Group A students to turn over their papers and read the directions at the top. Group A students should only read the directions at this point. Do not let them begin the exercise until they are told to do so.

5. When all of the Group A students have read the directions, have the Group B students turn their papers over. Have both groups begin the exercise and start the stopwatch.

6. Call out the elapsed times for students as they raise their hands signaling that they have completed the exercise.

7. At the end of five minutes, call "time," and instruct the students who have not completed the exercise to write "5 minutes" on their sheets.

8. Provide the answers but do not reveal the secret of the code: *[(1) The rock concert last Saturday was really great. (2) My uncle bought a new red sports car. (3) Every person in my family has a ton of freckles. (4) I enjoy playing video games with my friends. (5) During the game our coach became angry with the umpire.]*

9. Display **Visual 5.2**. Ask the Group A students to raise their hands if their time was between zero and one minute. Record in the first cell of the grid the number of students whose hands are raised. Continue to count the students and record numbers until the top portion of the chart is complete for both Group A students and Group B students.

10. (Optional) To demonstrate how experience can be a component of human capital, conduct

Round Two of the activity:

a. Distribute **Activity 5.2A** face down to the Group A students and **Activity 5.2B** face down to the Group B students. Start the clock, and have both groups read the directions and repeat the Exercise.

b. Provide the answers: *[(1) When my mom bakes bread, the whole house smells delicious. (2) At the park near my house there is a new soccer field. (3) Our garage is cluttered with old bikes and lawn mowers. (4) At the eighth grade dance our principal wore a tuxedo. (5) In science we learned how to separate hydrogen and oxygen.]*

c. Display **Visual 5.2** and complete the bottom portion, once again having the students comment on the results. *(Times may be more similar in this round, although Insiders may still perform more quickly because of their previous knowledge and experience.)*

11. Engage the students in a discussion of the differences between the scores of the two groups. Pose the questions shown at the bottom of **Visual 5.2**. *(Group A students were faster [more productive] because of knowledge of the code. Knowledge increases productivity. Experience [Round Two] usually increases the speed with which students solve the puzzles. So, experience increases productivity, too. Employers look for people with schooling [knowledge], experience, and a willingness to learn.).* In discussing these answers, teachers may wish to define productivity as an output/input ratio. An increase in productivity (the ratio) can be due to (1) a higher numerator with the same denominator or (2) a smaller denominator with the same numerator. (In this exercise, the increase in productivity of Group A is explained by the second reason: Group A members complete the same number of sentences in less time.)

12. Introduce the concept of "demand" as an important factor to be considered in career decisions. Explain that choosing a career should be based in part upon a person's interests and abilities, but it also should be based upon the demand for workers in certain occupations. Today, for example, the demand for workers who make and repair mechanical watches is very low; for that reason, it would probably not be a good idea for a young person to invest much time and effort in learning to make or repair watches, unless he or she wanted to do that sort of work as a hobby. However, young people would be wise to acquire skills, knowledge, and experience in fields of interest that are in high demand: computer technology, health care, engineering, accounting, etc.

13. Distribute a copy of **Exercise 5.1** from the *Student Workbook* to each student. Discuss the data shown on the exercise with the class. Ask the students to suggest reasons for the projected growth or decline in demand for various fields of work. *(Answers will vary, but the students should observe that occupations in technology and services are expected to be more abundant in the foreseeable future than occupations in manufacturing and agriculture. In the United States, demand for occupations that require more mental than physical labor seems to be growing.)*

14. Explain that knowing which occupational areas are expected to grow can help people plan the direction they will take in preparing for their careers. Aiming toward high-demand occupations may provide for more opportunities when the time comes to enter the world of work. Similarly, investing in human capital through education and training can make students more marketable in the workplace.

15. Emphasize this qualification: While it is very important for students to assess the demand for workers in various occupations, they should certainly consider their own interests, aptitudes, and goals as well. For example, even though the demand for agricultural workers may not be growing, people with certain kinds of human capital and interests are needed to replace workers in agriculture who leave their jobs or retire.

16. Turn back to **Exercise 5.1**. Divide the class into groups of four or five students and have them work together to calculate the projected change and the percent of projected increase or decrease in the occupational areas listed in **Exercise 5.1**. Students who are familiar with the use of spreadsheets might wish to use a computer to perform the calculations and to create graphs depicting the results. Given the length of this exercise, teachers may wish to assign different groups of students to calculate some portion of the table and share the results with the rest of the class. **(Answers are shown in Visual 5.3.)**

17. Have each student create a small poster depicting the projected change in one of the occupational areas. The poster should include a graph and a short paragraph expressing the student's interpretation of the data.

18. Review two main points of the lesson thus far: that investing in human capital and taking note of the demand for workers in certain occupations are important first steps toward making career choices. The next step is to do an occupational self-assessment.

19. Distribute a copy of **Exercise 5.2** to each student. Have the students complete the exercise, working independently. After they have analyzed their aptitudes for several career clusters, engage the class in a discussion of their surveys.

20. Turn to a consideration of skills. Explain that every job requires skills. Display **Visual 5.4**. Explain that the visual lists skills identified as important by the U.S. Department of Labor. Discuss the visual.

21. Point out that most employers spell out the skills and other requirements necessary for success in their companies. Sometimes the skills are specified in employment ads. Distribute a copy of **Exercise 5.3** from the *Student Workbook* to each student. Have the students read the ads in **Exercise 5.3** and discuss the skills required.

22. Have the students work independently to complete **Exercise 5.4**. Discuss the completed

exercise by reference to **Visual 5.4**. *(Answers will vary. Accept any responses that the students can logically defend. The letters the students write should adequately describe how their human capital satisfies the job requirements. Sample classified ad numbers for each skill include: Basic Skills [ad 1, 7, 8] Interpersonal Skills [ad 1, 4, 6], Teamwork [ad 2, 3, 4, 7], Use Technology [ad 1, 4, 5, 7, 8, 9, 10], Communication [ad 1, 3, 7, 8, 9, 10], Problem Solving [ad 5, 7, 9, 10], Good Work Ethic [ad 2, 10], Experience [ad 2, 5, 6, 8, 10], Organizational Skills [ad 2, 4, 6, 9].)*

23. Introduce entrepreneurship as a career possibility. Explain that choosing a career often means choosing to work for a small company or a big corporation, but it can also mean working for yourself. Define "entrepreneur" as a person who takes the risk and gathers the resources to provide a new or improved good or service to the marketplace. Mention a few well-known examples—Mary Kay Ash (Mary Kay Cosmetics), Steve Jobs (Apple Computer), or Sam Walton (Wal-Mart).

24. Display **Visual 5.5** and discuss its contents with the class. As necessary, clarify the main points—that entrepreneurs provide goods and services, adding variety and choice to the marketplace, and that entrepreneurs create new jobs. Explain, too, that all this involves risk. Some new businesses fail. And when people choose to work for themselves, one of their opportunity costs is the security of a guaranteed paycheck every week.

25. Distribute a copy of **Exercise 5.4** from the *Student Workbook* to each student. Have the students work in pairs to complete the exercise, answering questions 1, 2, and the Bonus question. *(Answers: A. Dimitrio would earn $3,510 a month at his old job, which would have included the value of his insurance and retirement. His expenses in his new business were $26,715 in July; therefore, he must have earned $30,225 in July to pay his expenses and pay himself $3,510. [$3510 + $26,715 = $30,225.] B. Answers will vary. If Dimitrio was tired of working for someone*

else, then running his own business and being his own boss might be best for him. However, when an entrepreneur assumes greater risk [of failing, not earning a profit], she or he probably expects, also, to gain a greater monetary reward. Dimitrio is not gaining a greater monetary return for assuming more risk, so perhaps in his case entrepreneurship is not worth the risk. Bonus: Dimitrio's salary was 11.6% of his July revenues. [$3,510 ÷ $30,225 = .1161 x 100 = 11.6%.].)

CLOSURE

Use the following questions to review the lesson:

- What is human capital? *(Human capital includes the knowledge, experience, skills, and attitudes that a person possesses or learns.)*

- What are some ways to develop your human capital? *(Education and work experience develop human capital.)*

- Why should you look at the demand for workers in an occupation when you consider a career choice? *(To determine whether it is likely that jobs will be available after you have prepared yourself to work in that occupation.)*

- What else should you consider when making a career choice? *(Your interests and aptitudes.)*

- What are some major differences between being an employee and being an entrepreneur? *(An employee works for someone else and does what the employer wants him or her to do. An entrepreneur chooses his or her work and may hire others to work in the business. Employees receive wages or salaries for their work; entrepreneurs take a risk and earn profits [or they lose money].)*

ASSESSMENT

Distribute a copy of **Lesson 5 Assessment** from the *Student Workbook* to each student; assign the students to complete the assessment, working independently. When they have completed the assignment, conduct a discussion of their work. In the discussion, have the students review the SCANS skills that Kelly did not exhibit. A sample answer key is provided in **Visual 5.6**. Students are likely to have different answers than are found on the key, so accept any responses that seem logical. Responses to the last section ("Give Kelly some advice . . . .") will vary. The students should list ways for Kelly to improve her SCANS skills through education, experience, and investment in her own human capital.

EXTENSION

Tell the students that it is now common for people to pursue a second career after they have retired or after they have decided that their initial career choice is no longer ideal. For example, some people become teachers after spending years in the financial services industry. You may wish to highlight someone in your school who has experienced a career change. Instruct students to search websites for articles providing guidance and tips for finding a second career. Have them note the first and second career individuals have chosen and list the transferrable skills that allowed the career transition.

What Is Human Capital?

Human capital includes the knowledge, skills, experience, and attitudes necessary for success.

Human Capital Needed for These Occupations:

Pilot	Marine Biologist	Web Designer	TV Reporter

Human Capital Score Sheet

		Group A	Group B
Round One	0:00 to 1:00 minute		
	1:01 to 2:00 minutes		
	2:01 to 3:00 minutes		
	3:01 to 4:00 minutes		
	4:01 to 5:00 minutes		
	5:00 max minutes		
Round Two **(the optional activity)**	0:00 to 1:00 minute		
	1:01 to 2:00 minutes		
	2:01 to 3:00 minutes		
	3:01 to 4:00 minutes		
	4:01 to 5:00 minutes		
	5:00 max minutes		

Questions

Who solved the codes faster? Why?

What can you say about the effect of information and knowledge on human capital?

If you completed Round 2, what can you say about the effect of experience on human capital?

FINANCIAL FITNESS FOR LIFE: Teacher Guide Grades 6-8
http://fffl.councilforeconed.org/6-8

Answer to Demand for Workers in Various Occupations

A: Industry	B: Actual # employed in 2006	C: Projected # employed in 2016	D: Change in Number (Column C – Column B) indicate + or -	E: Percent change (Column D/Column B x 100) indicate + or -
Registered nurses	2,505,000	3,092,000	587,000	23.4
Retail salesperson	4,477,000	5,034,000	557,000	12.4
Customer service rep	2,202,000	2,747,000	545,000	24.8
Food prep and serving	2,503,000	2,955,000	452,000	18.1
Office clerks	3,200,000	3,604,000	404,000	12.6
Personal & home care aides	767,000	1,156,000	389,000	50.7
Home health aides	787,000	1,171,000	384,000	48.8
Postsecondary teachers	1,672,000	2,054,000	382,000	22.8
Nursing aides, orderlies	1,447,000	1,711,000	264,000	18.2
Bookkeeping & accounting clerks	2,114,000	2,377,000	263,000	12.4
Waiters and waitresses	2,361,000	2,615,000	254,000	10.8
Child care workers	1,388,000	1,636,000	248,000	17.9
Administrative assistants	1,618,000	1,857,000	239,000	14.8
Computer software engineers	507,000	733,000	226,000	44.6
Accountants and auditors	1,274,000	1,500,000	226,000	17.7
Landscaping workers	1,220,000	1,441,000	221,000	18.1
Elementary school teachers	1,540,000	1,749,000	209,000	13.6
Receptionists and information clerks	1,173,000	1,375,000	202,000	17.2
Truck drivers, heavy & tractor-trailer	1,860,000	2,053,000	193,000	10.4
Maids and housekeeping cleaners	1,470,000	1,656,000	186,000	12.7
Security guards	1,040,000	1,216,000	176,000	16.9
Carpenters	1,462,000	1,612,000	150,000	10.3
Management analysts	678,000	827,000	149,000	22.0
Medical assistants	417,000	565,000	148,000	35.5
Computer systems analysts	504,000	650,000	146,000	29.0
Network systems analysts	262,000	402,000	140,000	53.4
Teacher assistants	1,312,000	1,449,000	137,000	10.4
Veterinarians	62,000	84,000	22,000	35.5
Financial analysts	221,000	295,000	74,000	33.5
Social & human service assistants	339,000	453,000	114,000	33.6
Physical therapy assistants	60,000	80,000	20,000	33.3
Pharmacy technicians	285,000	376,000	91,000	31.9
Forensic science technicians	13,000	17,000	4,000	30.8
Dental hygienists	167,000	217,000	50,000	29.9

Answer to Demand for Workers in Various Occupations

A: Industry	B: Actual # employed in 2006	C: Projected # employed in 2016	D: Change in Number (Column C – Column B) indicate + or -	E: Percent change (Column D/Column B x 100) indicate + or -
Mental health counselors	100,000	130,000	30,000	30.0
Dental assistants	280,000	362,000	82,000	29.3
Database administrators	119,000	154,000	35,000	29.4
Physical therapists	173,000	220,000	47,000	27.2
Manicurists and pedicurists	78,000	100,000	22,000	28.2
Environmental science protection techs	36,000	47,000	11,000	30.6
Physician assistants	66,000	83,000	17,000	25.8
Stock clerks and order fillers	1,705,000	1,574,000	-131,000	-7.7
Cashiers, except gaming	3,500,000	3,382,000	-118,000	-3.4
Packers and packagers, hand	834,000	730,000	-104,000	-12.5
File clerks	234,000	137,000	-97,000	-41.5
Farmers and ranchers	1,058,000	969,000	-89,000	-8.4
Order clerks	271,000	205,000	-66,000	-24.4
Sewing machine operators	233,000	170,000	-63,000	-27.0
Telemarketers	395,000	356,000	-39,00	-9.9
Computer operators	130,000	98,000	-32,000	-24.6
Word processors and typists	179,000	158,000	-21,000	-11.7
Computer programmers	435,000	417,000	-18,000	-4.1
Switchboard operators	177,000	163,000	-14,000	-7.9
Tile and marble setters	79,000	91,000	12,000	15.2
Plumbers, pipefitters, steamfitters	502,000	555,000	53,000	10.6
Firefighters	293,000	328,000	35,000	11.9
Medical equipment repairers	38,000	46,000	8,000	21.1
Embalmers	9,000	10,000	1,000	11.1
Nuclear medicine technologists	20,000	23,000	3,000	15.0
Paralegals and legal assistants	238,000	291,000	53,000	22.3
Cardiovascular technologists	45,000	57,000	12,000	26.7
Interior designers	72,000	86,000	14,000	19.4

Source: Bureau of Labor Statistics, Table 5. The 30 occupations with the largest employment growth, 2006-2016.Bureau of Labor Statistics, Table 6. The 30 fastest-growing occupations, 2006-2016. Bureau of Labor Statistics, Table 8. The 30 occupations with the largest employment declines, 2006-2016. Bureau of Labor Statistics, Table I-5. Above-average growth and above-average wage occupations, by educational attainment cluster and wages, 2006 and projected 2016. Note: these data are updated periodically, as part of the Bureau of Labor Statistics' Employment Projections program. For current updates, see www.bls.gov/news.release/ecopro.toc.htm.

FINANCIAL FITNESS FOR LIFE: Teacher Guide Grades 6-8
http://fffl.councilforeconed.org/6-8

SCANS Skills

The Secretary's Commission on Achieving Necessary Skills (SCANS) report, from the U.S. Department of Labor, presented a national model of skills that every worker needs in order to be productive and successful.

The SCANS skills include the following:

Basic Skills:
- Reading
- Writing
- Math
- Listening

Other Skills:
- Interpersonal skills
- Team work
- Use of technology and other resources
- Communication (oral and written)
- Problem solving
- Organizational skills
- Positive attitude/good work ethic

The SCANS list provides one set of terms for describing a person's "human capital": The knowledge, skills, experience and attitudes he or she may possess.

The Role of Entrepreneurs in the Economy

Entrepreneurs are innovators:

> They observe an opportunity.
>
> They create new goods and services.
>
> They improve existing products.

Entrepreneurs provide choice:

> They add goods and services to the marketplace.
>
> They offer variety.
>
> They design different approaches to familiar problems.

Entrepreneurs provide jobs:

> They hire workers for their businesses.
>
> They consume resources, thus providing jobs in the industries that supply those resources.

Entrepreneurs help the economy grow.

FINANCIAL FITNESS FOR LIFE: Teacher Guide Grades 6-8
http://fffl.councilforeconed.org/6-8

Lesson 5 Assessment: Answer Key

WHAT'S WRONG WITH THIS PICTURE?

Have the students complete **Lesson 5 Assessment** in the *Student Workbook*, working independently. (Sample answers are given below in bold.)

Read the story below, and underline every statement that illustrates habits that will NOT prepare Kelly for a successful career. HINT: You should find more than 12 mistakes. Then, above each incorrect statement, write the letter of the SCANS skill that Kelly is lacking.

Choose from these SCANS skills:

A. Reading, writing and math

B. Interpersonal skills

C. Teamwork

D. Use of technology

E. Oral communication

F. Problem solving

G. Good work ethic/on time/good attitude

H. Organizational skills

Kelly is a seventh-grader at Middleville Middle School. Her first class begins at 8:05, so she sets her alarm for 7:30. That way she's out of the kitchen door at 7:50 and **ready for her 20-minute walk to school. (G)** Yesterday, when she entered the building, she saw the principal, Ms. Ramirez.

"Yo," (E) Kelly shouted. "What's happenin'?"

"You're late, Kelly," said the principal, frowning.

"Whatever!" (E) replied Kelly, and she raced down the hall.

In class, Kelly ruffled through her book bag but **could not find any pens, pencils, or paper. (H)** When Mr. Choy asked for her math assignment, she didn't have that either.

"You'll have to go to the office," Mr. Choy told her.

In the principal's office, Kelly was asked to answer the phone while one of the secretaries stepped out. When the phone rang, Kelly picked it up.

"Hey, man, this is Middleville school. Whaddya want?" (E) she said.

The caller hung up, but Kelly could not figure out why. She decided to leave a note for the secretary. It said: **"Deer Sekretery, Somebody called and hung up. I don't no who it was." (A)**

When the phone rang again, Kelly picked it up and said, **"Whooze zis?" (E)**

"Please have Ms. Ramirez call the superintendent's office by 9:30," the caller said.

"Okay, okay," Kelly said. On a piece of scrap paper she wrote: "Ms. Ramirez - **go to the custodian's office after 9:30." (A)**

"Kelly, you need to keep a good record of the calls," said the school clerk.

"You can't tell me what to do," shouted Kelly. **"I'm doin' ya a favor by helpin' ya out." (B)**

The next day when Kelly woke up, it was dark in her bedroom. She flipped the switch about ten times, but her lamp would not light.

"Hey, what's wrong with my lamp?" she yelled to her mother.

"Maybe the bulb burned out," her mother suggested.

"Oh, I never thought of that," (F) said Kelly.

Kelly had not done her homework, so she decided not to go to school. **"Let's see, that's 15 days absent so far this year. That ain't too bad." (G)**

When Kelly returned to school her social studies teacher, Ms. Musielewicz, sent her to the computer lab to do some research for a big project. In the lab, Kelly was clueless. **She did not even know how to turn on the computer. (D)** The lab assistant tried to help her, but Kelly just shrugged.

"I took that stupid computer class last year, but I didn't like it. Besides, I'm gonna be a mechanic when I'm done with school**. I don't need no computer skills." (E)**

Finally, it was the last period of the day—gym class. The substitute teacher was assigning the students to teams for basketball. When Kelly got the ball, she dribbled down the floor and tried to shoot, even though she was surrounded by players from the other team.

"Pass. Pass the ball!" shouted the teacher.

But Kelly just tried to shoot again, and she was blocked by another player. Every time she got the ball, Kelly tried to shoot. **She never passed to another player. (C)**

When the bell rang at the end of the day, Kelly grabbed her book bag and ran out of the building. On the way home she stopped at the store and bought a candy bar for 55 cents, giving the clerk a $1 bill.

"With tax, that's 59 cents. Your change is 31 cents," the cashier said, handing Kelly a quarter, a nickel and a penny.

"Hey," said another shopper. "That's not the right change."

"Sure it is," shrugged Kelly. **"It must be. The man said it was." (A)**

When Kelly got home, her mother asked how things went at school.

"All right, I guess," she replied. "But I can't wait to finish school and get a job. Then I can do anything I want."

Give Kelly some advice for how to improve her human capital and increase her chances for a successful career.

FINANCIAL FITNESS FOR LIFE: Teacher Guide Grades 6-8
http://fffl.councilforeconed.org/6-8

Success Depends Upon Human Capital (Group A)

Each sentence below is written in code. CLUE: The last word in the mixed-up sentence is the first word in the real sentence. The first word in the mixed-up sentence is the second word in the real sentence. (Example: If the mixed-up sentence is **Prefer butter instead candy of cookies peanut I**, the real sentence would be **I prefer peanut butter cookies instead of candy**. The words are numbered below to show you how it works.)

2	4	6	8	7	5	3	1
prefer	butter	instead	candy	of	cookies	peanut	I

Rewrite the deciphered message below each coded message. Raise your hand when you are finished; when your teacher calls out your time, write the time in the blank at the bottom of the page.

Rock last was great really Saturday concert the.

Uncle a red car sports new bought my.

Person my has ton freckles of a family in every.

Enjoy video with friends my games playing I.

The our became with umpire the angry coach game during.

My Time: _____

Success Depends Upon Human Capital (Group B)

Each sentence below is written in code. Figure out the code and decipher the sentences. Rewrite the deciphered sentence below each coded sentence. Raise your hand when you are finished; when your teacher calls out your time, write it in the blank at the bottom of the page.

Rock last was great really Saturday concert the.

Uncle a red car sports new bought my.

Person my has ton freckles of a family in every.

Enjoy video with friends my games playing I.

The our became with umpire the angry coach game during.

My Time: _____

FINANCIAL FITNESS FOR LIFE: Teacher Guide Grades 6-8
http://fffl.councilforeconed.org/6-8

Success Depends Upon Human Capital (Group A)

Each sentence below is written in code. CLUE: The last word in the mixed-up sentence is the first word in the real sentence. The first word in the mixed-up sentence is the second word in the real sentence. (Example: If the mixed-up sentence is **Prefer butter instead candy of cookies peanut I**, the real sentence would be **I prefer peanut butter cookies instead of candy**. The words are numbered below to show you how it works.)

2	4	6	8	7	5	3	1
prefer	butter	instead	candy	of	cookies	peanut	I

Rewrite the deciphered message below each coded message. Raise your hand when you are finished; when your teacher calls out your time, write the time in the blank at the bottom of the page.

My bakes the house delicious smells whole bread mom when.

The near house is new field soccer a there my park at.

Garage cluttered old and mowers lawn bikes with is our.

The grade our wore tuxedo a principal dance eighth at.

Science learned to hydrogen oxygen and separate how we in.

My Time: _____

Success Depends Upon Human Capital (Group B)

Each sentence below is written in code. Figure out the code and decipher the sentences. Rewrite the deciphered sentence below each coded sentence. Raise your hand when you are finished; when your teacher calls out your time, write it in the blank at the bottom of the page.

My bakes the house delicious smells whole bread mom when.

The near house is new field soccer a there my park at.

Garage cluttered old and mowers lawn bikes with is our.

The grade our wore tuxedo a principal dance eighth at.

Science learned to hydrogen oxygen and separate how we in.

My Time: _____

Productivity

LESSON DESCRIPTION AND BACKGROUND

The students examine ways to develop their human capital. They discover that they make themselves more productive by developing their human capital and by using capital resources, the tools of their trade. As they become more productive, they become more valuable to employers. As they become more valuable to employers, they gain earning power, thus improving their standard of living.

Lesson 6 is correlated with national standards for mathematics and economics, and with personal finance guidelines, as shown in Tables 1-3 in the introductory section of this publication.

ECONOMIC AND PERSONAL FINANCE CONCEPTS

- Capital resources
- Human capital
- Productivity
- Wage

OBJECTIVES

At the end of this lesson, the student will be able to:

- Give examples of **capital resources** used in various careers.
- Explain ways in which **productivity** can be increased.
- Explain ways in which the use of **capital resources** increases **productivity**.
- Identify the **human capital** required for particular jobs.
- Explain how certain skills are acquired.

TIME REQUIRED

One 45-minute class period

MATERIALS

- A transparency of **Visual 6.1**, **6.2**, and **6.3**
- A copy for each student of the **Introduction** and **Vocabulary** sections for **Lesson 6** from the *Student Workbook*
- A copy for each student of **Exercise 6.1** from the *Student Workbook*
- A copy for each student of **Lesson 6 Assessment** from the *Student Workbook*
- Calculators
- A clock with a second hand for students to access

ADDITIONAL RESOURCES

To download visuals, find related lessons, correlations to state standards, interactives, and more, visit http://fffl.councilforeconed.org/6-8/lesson6.

PROCEDURE

1. Begin the lesson by asking the students to read the Introduction and Vocabulary sections for **Lesson 6** in the *Student Workbook*. Then explain that many adults work very hard at their jobs. And many others—those temporarily unemployed, for example—would like to work hard. Ask: Why do people work so hard? What do workers receive in return for their work? ***(Responses will vary. Suggest a two-part summary: Overall returns from working might include intangible benefits such as self-gratification and self-esteem; the economic returns from working are wages and benefits.)***

2. Observe further that some workers earn more, in wages and benefits, than others. Introduce the concept of "productivity" as a factor related to earnings. Display **Visual 6.1**. Use the visual to explain that some workers are more

productive than others, and more productive workers are more valuable to employers than other, less productive workers. Point out that Yolanda considered Mike to be more productive than Chris because Mike could accomplish more work than Chris in the same amount of time.

3. How might employees increase their productivity? Display the first part of **Visual 6.2**. Use the visual to explain that employees can increase their productivity by using "capital resources." Capital resources are goods produced for the purpose of producing other goods and services. A hammer is an example of a capital resource; so is a computer. Hammers and computers enable workers to produce other goods and services—the wood trim needed for a new home, the documents needed for the operation of insurance companies, hospitals, accounting firms, and many other organizations.

4. Explain that capital resources include tools, machinery and buildings. Ask:

a. What capital resources might be used by a doctor? *(Certain tools—e.g., a stethoscope, a computer; also certain buildings—e.g., clinics, hospitals.)*

b. What capital resources might be used by a police officer? *(Again, certain tools—e.g., a squad car, radio, weapon, handcuffs; also certain buildings—e.g., a police station, a courthouse.)*

5. Display the rest of **Visual 6.2**. Explain that employees can also increase their productivity by developing their "human capital." Human capital is the combination of knowledge, skills, health, experience, and attitudes that a worker acquires over time. The development of human capital enhances an employee's value as a worker. Suggest a way for the students to imagine this: On the day you were born, you were given a large, empty box; as you have grown older and have learned many new things, you have added a great deal of knowledge and skills to be placed in the box.

6. Invite the students to elaborate on this point. Ask: What skills have you placed into this box at this point in your lives? *(Possibilities include reading skills, math skills, social skills, critical thinking skills, athletic skills, child-care skills, cooking skills, etc.)* Explain that this is only the beginning. They will acquire many other skills by the time they set about looking for their first full-time job. At that time, they will present their skill sets to their employers as if they were offering their employers a gift box of skills that the employers could use to build their businesses.

7. Explain that the quality of workers' human capital will likely determine the workers' levels of income. In general, people who are better educated and more highly skilled are more valuable as employees. Employers compensate workers in large measure according to the knowledge and skills they bring to their jobs.

8. Introduce the concept of "investing" in "human capital." When people take steps to improve their human capital—e.g., by mastering the uses of a new software program or by completing an electrician's training program—we say they are investing in their human capital. In this expression, "investing" refers to spending time, effort, and perhaps money now in order to gain something that will be valuable in the future.

9. Emphasize the point that human capital is related to "productivity." Recall that Mike was more productive at cutting grass than Chris was. Pose a hypothetical situation: Suppose that Mike and Chris were not in business together, but were competing for the same $8.00-per-hour grass-cutting job. Which of the boys would get the job? *(For jobs where grass-cutting productivity is the deciding factor, Mike would be more likely to be hired.)*

10. Suggest that the information on **Visual 6.1** might not tell the whole story about Mike and Chris's grass-cutting service. Distribute a copy of **Exercise 6.1** to each student. Ask them to read the exercise and answer questions 1 and 2. Discuss the students' answers. *(1. Chris had social and business skills that he used in approaching customers and marketing the grass-cutting service. 2. Mike was more productive*

at cutting grass; Chris was more productive at managing the business. The two boys had different personal qualities and skills, making each one better suited for some aspects of their work and less suited for others.)

11. Tell the students that, to conclude this lesson, they will participate in an activity that illustrates two ways of improving productivity.

a. Display **Visual 6.3**. Explain that the activity, called Give and Take, will make use of a math exercise to demonstrate productivity. In this exercise, the students begin with a number and multiply it by 2 to get a product. Then they multiply the product by 3, then by 4, and so on, until they reach the final multiplier assigned by the teacher. Then they divide that final product by 2, then 3, then 4, and so on until they reach the number initially used in the multiplication. Point out this scheme on the visual.

b. Separate the students into teams of two students each. Ask one student in each team to act as timekeeper and one to volunteer to do a Give and Take. Depending on how much time you have available and the skill level of your students, give the volunteers a starting number of one or two digits and have them multiply by 2, 3, 4, and so on, up to the number you designate; then begin dividing by 2, 3, 4, and so on, up to the number you designate. Do not exceed 10 as the multiplier.

c. Instruct each volunteer's partner to time him or her and record the amount of minutes and seconds it takes the volunteer to complete the Give and Take correctly. Do not allow calculators.

d. When all volunteers have completed the Give and Take, instruct them to do the exact same problem again. Have the timekeepers record the time it takes for completion of this round of calculations. The students will probably complete the calculations in less time than they needed in the first round.

e. Ask: What made the difference? *(Discuss responses. As necessary, clarify the point that*

the students were able to complete their calculations more quickly this time because they had developed some skill for the task through practice. Human capital can be enhanced through practice. The more you practice a skill, the better you will become. Employers recognize this. When you are newly employed, your employer will probably assume that you will need time to develop your productivity. With practice doing the job, you will become more proficient.)

f. Now give the volunteers calculators. Explain that you want to find out how much difference the use of this capital resource can make in the students' productivity. Once again, have the timekeepers record the time it takes the partners to complete the calculations. If time permits, allow the students to do this exercise twice, to demonstrate once again the value of "practice" and "capital resources" in improving productivity.

CLOSURE

Use the following questions to review the lesson.

- What is human capital? *(The combination of knowledge, skills, health, talent, and attitudes that enhances your value as a worker.)*

- Why does investment in your human capital increase your possibility for more income in the future? *(Employers are willing to pay more for more skilled, knowledgeable, talented, and healthy workers because they are more productive.)*

- How do capital resources increase productivity? *(Capital resources allow workers to get work done more efficiently. They do this by allowing workers to produce more output in the same amount of time, or by producing the same amount of output in less time.)*

• How can you increase your human capital? *(Answers will vary, but students should recognize that they must acquire education, practice their skills, and develop their talents.)*

ASSESSMENT

Distribute a copy of **Lesson 6 Assessment** from the *Student Workbook* to each student. Assign the students to complete the assessment task. Establish a due date. Evaluate the assignments for completeness and for the extent to which the work shows understanding of the concepts emphasized in this lesson.

EXTENSION

Have small groups of students think about a process that could be improved. It could be a new production method in transportration (e.g. a new kind of car or train; shoes with springs or rockets, etc.), communication, agriculture or some other sector. Instruct the groups to construct a poster with a schematic or picture of their idea. Have each group present their ideas to the class.

The Story of Mike and Chris

Mike and Chris had a grass-cutting business. Week after week, Mike and Chris cut the grass at a ball field. They had identical lawn mowers, began cutting at the same time, and worked for two hours.

However, when they were through cutting the ball field, Mike had cut three-fourths of the field while Chris had cut only one-fourth. The ball field owner, Yolanda, commended Mike for his productivity.

Capital Resources and Human Capital

- Capital resources are goods produced for the purpose of producing other goods and services. For instance, hammers are produced to aid in construction. Using a hammer to pound something is much more effective than using a rock. A hammer increases the productivity of construction workers.

- Human capital is the combination of knowledge, skills, health, talents, and attitudes that a worker obtains over time. Knowing how to use new equipment and efficient procedures increases productivity. The development of your human capital enhances your value as a worker.

FINANCIAL FITNESS FOR LIFE: Teacher Guide Grades 6-8
http://fffl.councilforeconed.org/6-8

Give and Take

$2 \times 2 = \boxed{4}$

$4 \times 3 = \boxed{12}$

$12 \times 4 = \boxed{48}$

$48 \times 5 = \boxed{240}$

$240 \div 2 = \boxed{120}$

$120 \div 3 = \boxed{40}$

$40 \div 4 = \boxed{10}$

$10 \div 5 = \boxed{2}$

Managing Cash

LESSON DESCRIPTION AND BACKGROUND

Although most middle school and junior high students do not hold full-time jobs, many of them have money to spend, often from an allowance or a part-time job. As a group, they have discretionary income that totals, by some estimates, billions of dollars a year. Yet, while teens tend to be prolific consumers, most do not have a plan, or budget, for sensible spending and saving. This lesson challenges students to create a reasonable spending plan based on an appropriate allocation of income in a number of categories, such as clothing, entertainment, and food.

Lesson 7 is correlated with national standards for mathematics and economics, and with personal finance guidelines, as shown in Tables 1-3 in the introductory section of this publication.

ECONOMIC AND PERSONAL FINANCE CONCEPTS

- Budget (or spending plan)
- Fixed expenses
- Opportunity cost
- Periodic or occasional expenses
- Periodic income
- Planned expense
- Trade-off
- Unplanned expense
- Variable expenses

OBJECTIVES

At the end of this lesson, the student will be able to:

- Distinguish between **fixed**, **variable**, and **occasional expenses**, as well as **planned** and **unplanned expenses**.
- Record and analyze expenses.
- Develop a **spending plan**.

- Evaluate how well a **spending plan** is kept based on expenses and income for a period.

TIME REQUIRED

Two 45-minute class periods, plus out-of-class time for the spending-plan activities (see **Procedures 7** and **12**)

MATERIALS

- A transparency of **Visual 7.1** and **Visual 7.2**

- A copy for each student of **Introduction to Theme 3** and **Introduction** and **Vocabulary** sections of **Lesson 7** from the *Student Workbook*

- A copy for each student of **Exercise 7.1** and **Exercise 7.2** from the *Student Workbook*

- A copy for each student of **Lesson 7 Assessment** from the *Student Workbook*

- Calculators

ADDITIONAL RESOURCES

To download visuals, find related lessons, correlations to state standards, interactives, and more, visit http://fffl.councilforeconed.org/6-8/lesson7.

PROCEDURE

1. Distribute a copy of **Introduction to Theme 3** and **Introduction** and **Vocabulary** sections of **Lesson 7** in the *Student Workbook* to each student. Have the students review the handouts and discuss them briefly, if necessary. Introduce the lesson by asking the students to name important events that families and friends celebrate together. Make a list on the board as the students suggest events. *(The students will probably name birthdays, weddings, family reunions, anniversaries, graduations, holidays, and religious events.)*

2. Ask the students what it is that families plan for in these events. On the board, list the students' ideas next to the events. *(The students will probably suggest decorations, food, gifts, seating arrangements, entertainment, etc.)*

3. Engage the students in a discussion of how planning is important to the success of any event. Without planning, what might go wrong? *(Encourage the suggestion of big blunders and oversights.)*

4. Explain that planning is important in money matters, too. For example:

a. How do people pull together enough money to make a down payment for an automobile or a home? *(By planned saving.)*

b. How do people make sure they will have enough money to cover expenses for the entire month? *(By planning carefully for what can be spent throughout the month.)*

5. Pick up on discussion of the latter problem—planning for spending throughout a month's time. Explain that managing cash requires people to examine how they earn money and how they spend it. A cash flow statement is one way of recording how money is spent—what a person has purchased, the amount, and whether the expense was planned or unplanned.

6. Display **Visual 7.1**. Discuss "fixed," "variable" and "occasional expenses," and "planned" versus "unplanned expenses." Ask the students which expenses are more subject to control by the consumer *(variable)*. Note that planned expenses may include both variable and fixed expenses. Ask the students to think of some examples to add to each of the categories. *(Answers might include such things—placed in their proper categories—as a fixed monthly parking fee, money spent on attending sporting events, club dues, etc.)*

7. Distribute a copy of **Exercise 7.1** from the *Student Workbook* to each student. Review the form with the students, noting the categories for food, clothing, entertainment, or other. Ask the students to keep track of their expenditures for

one week, using this form. Point out the sample line on the form where the expenditure is named (item/service) and the cost is listed in the food column. Each item is further marked as fixed or variable and whether it was a planned or unplanned purchase.

8. Emphasize the importance of recording every expenditure, no matter how small, and explain that when the students choose to spend money for one item, their "opportunity cost" is the next-best use they could have made of that money.

9. At the end of the week, have the students total their expenditures (using calculators or paper and pencil) and record the totals for each category (food, clothing, entertainment, or other) on **Exercise 7.1**. Then have them total all expenditures for a Grand Total. Have the students recalculate the totals by adding all the planned expenses together, and then all the unplanned expenses. Students can also calculate how much they spend on fixed and variable expenses. Students may also wish to think about how many items represented periodic expenses.

10. Have the students calculate the percentage of the grand total accounted for by each category. Explain how to calculate percentages. [Divide each expense by Total Expenses (the Grand Total) and then multiply by 100. For example: (Amount spent for Food ÷ Total Expenses) x 100 = % spent for Food.]

11. Discuss the answers to the questions in **Exercise 7.1**. *(Answers will vary. Students should note that variable expenses are the easiest to decrease.)*

12. Optional: Have the students develop a spending plan for the next week. During that week they should record their expenses as before. At the end of the week, ask the students to evaluate how well they stayed within their spending plans. Discuss what changes they could make to improve their spending plan for the next week.

13. Explain that the students' experience with their spending plans resembles, on a small scale,

an experience that is common in the adult world—that is, the challenge of living within one's means. Financial advisors often examine the income and expense statements of individuals in order to help them determine whether their spending habits are reasonable. Distribute a copy of **Exercise 7.2** from the *Student Workbook* to each student. Divide the class into groups of four or five students and assign each group to read one case study from the exercise. Within their groups, students should total the expenses and compare total expenses to monthly income; then they should answer Questions 1-4 and report their answers to the class. You may wish to note that in this example, savings is what is left over after all expenses are accounted for. Many financial experts advise people to treat savings differently by "paying themselves first." This means, in effect, making savings a spending category. You can point out to the students that, to some extent, this is being done in **Exercise 7.2** when each person makes a monthly contribution to their retirement plan. *(Calculations are shown in Visual 7.2. Answers to Questions 1-4 will vary.)*

14. Have the students answer Questions 5-9 on **Exercise 7.2**. Discuss the answers. *(5. Jeff; 6. Brian and Maria; 7. Lauren and Suzanne; 8. $44. 9. Answers will vary; the students might suggest that Lauren should reduce her entertainment, phone, clothes, charity, or contributions to retirement plan to come up with $600.)*

CLOSURE

Divide the class into three groups (A-C) and have them assume these roles:

- Group A: those who receive the same salary each week—e.g., from an allowance

- Group B: those who receive a regular allowance plus periodic income—e.g., from occasional jobs

- Group C: those who have only periodic income—no regular allowance, only occasional jobs such as baby sitting, mowing lawns, etc.

The students in each group should answer the following questions from the point of view of their group's type of worker:

- How do you estimate your income?

- How do you estimate your expenses?

- What is the hardest part about setting up your spending plan?

- How do fixed, variable, and occasional expenses affect your spending plan?

- How do you handle emergencies that cause increases in expenses?

- What advice about spending plans would you give to people who have the same type of income sources that you have?

ASSESSMENT

Have the students complete **Lesson 7 Assessment**, working independently. (Answers are given below.)

- *James Bond's expenses are less than his income; he has $538 left over. His total income is $1,974,654. His total expenses are $1,974,116.*

- *Answers may vary, but the students should respond that his opportunity cost is the best alternative use of $175,000 that he must give up in order to buy the new plane. Perhaps he'll have to give up the maintenance of his home in Hawaii.*

- *Fifteen percent of Bond's income is $296,198.10, so he'll have to create a current savings plan to follow the recommendation of his financial advisor. Bond's trade-off might be that he'll have to spend less on other things, such as airplane tickets, restaurant meals, etc. Bond may note that he is currently allocating $165,987 of his income as a retirement contribution.*

EXTENSION

Explain that nearly all expenses can be budgeted; however, unplanned expenses, by definition, are not specifically placed in a spending plan. Sudden car or household repairs often drive people to payday lenders because they have failed to plan for unplanned expenses. One approach to this problem is to anticipate unplanned expenses. If you have an old car, you can anticipate car repairs. If you get a speeding ticket you can anticipate an increase in your insurance premiums.

Instruct the students to write a list of possible unplanned expenses that might lie ahead during their high school years and brainstorm ways they can build an emergency fund. This might include placing a few dollars of weekly allowance, a percentage of the pay for chores, or half of all gift money in a savings account.

Ways to Categorize Expenses

Fixed Expenses

Spending that remains the same from month to month.

Examples:
- Rent or mortgage payments
- Car payments

Variable Expenses

Spending that changes from month to month.

Examples:
- Cell phone bill
- Gas for the car
- Food purchased at restaurants

Occasional or Periodic Expenses

Expenses that occur once or a few times a year.

Examples:
- Medical/dental check-ups
- Property taxes
- Car maintenance

Planned Expenses

Spending you expect, and for which you plan.

Examples:
- New clothing
- Friday night movie and ice cream
- Dues for a fitness club

Unplanned Expenses

Spending for an emergency, an urgent need, or an impulse purchase.

Examples:
- Car repairs resulting from an accident
- Visit to a doctor for a sprained ankle or appendectomy
- Donation to a collection for victims of an earthquake

FINANCIAL FITNESS FOR LIFE: Teacher Guide Grades 6-8
http://fffl.councilforeconed.org/6-8

Living within Their Means: Answers to Exercise 7.2

Case Study A

Lauren earns $51,300 annually

She earns $4,275 monthly

Contribution to retirement plan	$240
Rent/home mortgage	780
Utilities	340
Phone/cable/Internet	180
Food/groceries	300
Car payment	660
Insurance (car/rental/home)	188
Transportation, incl. gas	168
Charity	92
Clothes	66
Loan payments	540
Entertainment	240
Services (cleaning, hair stylist)	180
Other	166
Total Monthly Expenses	$4,140

Did Lauren spend more or less than she earned? ___**LESS**___ By how much? __**$135**__

Living within Their Means: Answers to Exercise 7.2

Case Study B

Brian's annual income is $42,000

His monthly income is $3,500

Contribution to retirement plan	$222
Rent/home mortgage	870
Utilities	288
Phone/cable/Internet	210
Food/groceries	290
Car payment	438
Insurance (car/rental/home)	178
Transportation, incl. gas	105
Charity	107
Clothes	138
Loan payments	368
Entertainment	180
Services	150
Other	222
Total Monthly Expenses	$3,766

Did Brian spend more or less than he earned? ___**MORE**___ By how much?__*$266*___

FINANCIAL FITNESS FOR LIFE: Teacher Guide Grades 6-8
http://fffl.councilforeconed.org/6-8

Living within Their Means: Answers to Exercise 7.2

Case Study C

Maria earns $44,000 annually.

She earns $3,667 monthly

Contribution to retirement plan	$120
Rent/home mortgage	690
Utilities	342
Phone/cable/Internet	270
Food/groceries	450
Car payment	150
Insurance (car/rental/home)	264
Transportation, incl. gas	96
Charity	24
Clothes	222
Loan payments	728
Entertainment	198
Services (cleaning, hair stylist)	90
Other	180
Total Monthly Expenses	$3,824

Did Maria spend more or less than she earned? _____**MORE**_____ By how much? ___**$157**___

Living within Their Means: Answers to Exercise 7.2

Case Study D

Suzanne earns $160,000 annually

She earns $13,333 monthly

Contribution to retirement plan	$1,780
Rent/home mortgage	4,804
Utilities	670
Phone/cable/Internet	324
Food/groceries	336
Car payment	900
Insurance (car/rental/home)	750
Transportation, incl. gas	450
Charity	670
Clothes	270
Loan payments	900
Entertainment	540
Services (cleaning, hair stylist)	438
Other	306
Total Monthly Expenses	$13,138

Did Suzanne spend more or less than she earned? _____*LESS*_____ By how much? ___*$195*___

FINANCIAL FITNESS FOR LIFE: Teacher Guide Grades 6-8
http://fffl.councilforeconed.org/6-8

Living within Their Means: Answers to Exercise 7.2

Case Study E

Marcus earns $80,400 annually

He earns $6,700 monthly

Contribution to retirement plan	$ 780
Rent/home mortgage	1,529
Utilities	342
Phone/cable/Internet	114
Food/groceries	409
Car payment	420
Insurance (car/rental/home)	225
Transportation, incl.gas	102
Charity	114
Clothes	180
Loan payments	1,661
Entertainment	342
Services (cleaning, hair stylist)	114
Other	324
Total Monthly Expenses	$6,656

Did Marcus spend more or less than he earned? _____**LESS**_____ By how much? _____**$44**_____

Living within Their Means: Answers to Exercise 7.2

Case Study F

Jeff earns $40,400 annually

He earns $3,367 monthly

Contribution to retirement plan	$240
Rent/home mortgage	900
Utilities	78
Phone/cable/Internet	54
Food/groceries	336
Car payment	186
Insurance (car/rental/home)	138
Transportation, incl. gas	168
Charity	66
Clothes	48
Loan payments	714
Entertainment	54
Services (cleaning, hair stylist)	72
Other	90
Total Monthly Expenses	$3,144

Did Jeff spend more or less than he earned? _____**LESS**_____ By how much? ____**$223**____

FINANCIAL FITNESS FOR LIFE: Teacher Guide Grades 6-8
http://ffffl.councilforeconed.org/6-8

Choosing and Using a Checking Account

LESSON DESCRIPTION AND BACKGROUND

The students learn the fundamentals of maintaining a checking account. They examine electronic banking methods, the writing of checks, and using a check register. They examine the features and costs of checking accounts, in preparation for the time when they acquire checking accounts of their own.

Lesson 8 is correlated with national standards for mathematics and economics, and with personal finance guidelines, as shown in Tables 1-3 in the introductory section of this publication.

ECONOMIC AND PERSONAL FINANCE CONCEPTS

- ATM card
- Checking account
- Checkbook register
- Credit union
- Debit card
- Direct Deposit
- Online banking
- Overdraft

OBJECTIVES

At the end of this lesson, the student will be able to:

- Identify major features, benefits, and costs of **checking accounts**.
- Explain the responsibilities that come with having a checking account.
- Write a check correctly.
- Describe **ATM cards**, **debit cards**, **direct deposit**, and automatic withdrawals.
- Identify safety precautions for use with ATM machines.

TIME REQUIRED

Two 45-minute class periods

MATERIALS

- A transparency of **Visual 8.1**, **8.2**, **8.3**, **8.4**, and **8.5**

- A copy for each student of **Introduction** and **Vocabulary** sections of **Lesson 8** from the *Student Workbook*

- A copy for each student of **Exercise 8.1** and **8.2** from the *Student Workbook*

- A copy for each student of **Reading 8.1**, **8.2**, and **8.3** from the *Student Workbook*

- A copy for each student of **Lesson 8 Assessment** from the *Student Workbook*

ADDITIONAL RESOURCES

To download visuals, find related lessons, correlations to state standards, interactives, and more, visit http://fffl.councilforeconed.org/6-8/lesson8.

PROCEDURE

1. Distribute a copy of the **Introduction** and **Vocabulary** sections of **Lesson 8** from the *Student Workbook* to each student. Ask the students to read this handout and introduce the lesson's focus on checking accounts. Explain that the students will learn about the advantages of checking accounts, how to maintain a checking account, and the different institutions that offer checking accounts.

2. Point out that checking accounts are useful financial tools. It usually is not important for a middle school student to have a checking account, but as soon as a young person gets a job, a checking account becomes nearly essential. In anticipation of that time, the stu-

dents should know how to maintain a checking account. This will prepare them to track their spending, to manage their personal finances, and to build good credit standing.

3. Distribute a copy of **Reading 8.1** from the *Student Workbook* to each student; ask the students to read the information it presents. Discuss the reading. Ask:

a. Why would using checks or a debit card for payments be safer and more convenient than using cash? *(Cash can be lost or stolen; you can't prove you've made a payment in cash without having a receipt; writing checks and using debit cards helps you keep track of your expenditures; debit cards are convenient to carry and use; in some checking accounts, money on deposit earns interest.)*

b. What costs could you incur by using a checking account? *(Fees for printed checks, fees for overdrafts [checks written on an overdrawn account], monthly service charges, or a charge for each check you write.)*

4. Refer the students again to **Reading 8.1**. Review the features and costs of checking accounts. Assign the students to call a bank, credit union, or savings institution in their community and ask about the types of checking accounts these institutions offer. Have them seek answers to the questions posed in the reading. Remind them that most of these institutions are not open in the evening, so they will need to place their calls right after school. Explain that they will make a brief report on their findings.

5. Now that the students understand some key features of checking accounts and have identified a local financial institution that offers these accounts, it is time for them to learn about the basic steps in opening a checking account. Distribute a copy of **Reading 8.2** from the *Student Workbook* to each student and ask them to read through the steps involved in opening a checking account. Some of the students may already have a relationship with a bank. It is common for parents to open up a youth savings account when children are young. Tell the students that for many of them, the next step they will take

with a financial institution will be to open a checking account. The procedures for doing this are found in this reading.

6. Turn to an increasingly important topic in personal finance: Electronic and online access to checking accounts. Explain that writing checks and completing paper deposit tickets are no longer the only ways to access a checking account. Today, most account holders access their accounts by using ATMs and via online banking. Ask:

a. What is an "ATM"? **(The students will probably say that it is a machine located in malls, airports, and banks where customers can withdraw money from their accounts. This answer is correct, so far as it goes. But the students also should know that ATM stands for Automated Teller Machine, and that ATMs have several functions, such as allowing the account holder to transfer money from one account to another, to check an account balance, or to deposit money.)**

b. What is an "ATM card"? *(It is an identification card that allows the holder to withdraw money from his or her account at an ATM. A personal identification number [PIN], along with the card, is required for transactions.)*

7. Explain that providing access to accounts via ATM machines is only one of several electronic banking services. Display **Visual 8.1**. Explain each of the electronic methods as follows:

a. A bit more about ATMs: These machines can be used at all hours of the day or night. Customers may use them to make deposits or withdrawals from their accounts, verify their account balances, and transfer money from one account to another. Customers may also use other banks' ATMs, but they should be careful in doing so. Other banks may charge a fee for the use of their machines. Customers also should be cautious using ATMs for another reason. Crimes of theft and fraud associated with the use of ATMs have been reported. Customers should therefore use care when they withdraw or deposit cash at an ATM. Distribute a copy of **Reading 8.3** to each student; have the students read it to learn about additional safety precautions. Suggest that the students might share this information with their parents.

b. The "debit card" enables account holders to use another method of electronic payment. (The card used at ATM machines is usually the same one used as a debit card.) A debit card looks like a credit card. A customer using a debit card (at a store or a restaurant, for example) swipes the card in making a purchase, as if it were a credit card. The debit card is scanned and the customer enters a PIN or signature. No cash changes hands. But using a debit card differs from using a credit card in one very important way. When a customer uses a credit card, she takes out a "loan" from the card issuer and will be billed later for repayment of the loan. When a customer uses a debit card, he immediately transfers money, electronically, from his checking account to the merchant's account. Using a debit card is simple, fast, and convenient.

c. When using electronic banking services, customers must always remember to record the transactions in their check register. Display **Visual 8.2**. Explain that an account holder can keep a running balance of a checking account in the check register. Each time a check is written, the account holder can simply write in the date, the check number, to whom the check was written, and the amount of the check. The account holder deducts the amount of the check from the previous balance. This is very convenient because the pad of checks and the check register are contained in the same book. However, with electronic transactions, the check register may not be handy when the transaction occurs. The account holder then must remember to note the automatic deposits and withdrawals, as well as debit card transactions. Many banks provide access to checking accounts online, where customers can check their account

balance, view statements and payment records, transfer balances, and pay bills.

8. Ask the students if they've ever watched their parents sit down to pay the bills. Bills for goods and services—the telephone, cable TV, electricity, etc.—come every month. These bills can't be handled by debit cards or ATMs, so many consumers write out checks, address envelopes, pay postage, and make a trip to the post office to mail the checks off. However, there is an electronic alternative. Bank customers can use "online bill payment" for paying many of these bills. One method is to have the financial institution where you have an account pay your regularly-scheduled bills electronically from your account. Examples include monthly payments for rent, mortgages, and utilities. Another method allows the consumer to make payments electronically. Using this type of online banking, consumers can transfer funds from their accounts to other accounts in order to pay bills.

9. Money that bank customers receive regularly by check can be electronically transferred to the customers' accounts. This service is called direct deposit. People often use this service to deposit their paychecks; sometimes, direct deposit is required. Instead of receiving a paycheck, workers paid by direct deposit receive confirmation that their money has been deposited. There are several advantages to using direct deposit. They save trips to the bank to cash or deposit checks; they eliminate the possibility of losing the checks; and the money usually gets into the account sooner.

10. Turn to some matters of detail about using a checkbook. Ask the students if they have ever received a check as a gift, or if they have ever seen a check. If they have, they may remember what information a check contains. Distribute a copy of **Exercise 8.1** from the *Student Workbook* to each student. Instruct them to reproduce a check in the blank space provided. When the students have completed the task, display **Visual 8.3**. Have the students compare their versions with an image of a real check.

11. By reference to **Visual 8.3**, discuss check symbols and entries as follows:

- The information in the upper-left corner includes the name and address of the check writer. Often people have their phone number printed on their checks for convenience; however, this practice is no longer recommended because telephone numbers are sometimes useful to people engaged in identity theft.

- The number in the upper-right corner is the check number. Check numbers enable the check writer to keep track of the checks she or he writes.

- The Date line provides a space for recording the date on which a check is written. Check writers must be sure to have enough money in their accounts to cover the checks on the day the checks are written. It is unwise to write a check based on the anticipation of a deposit that will take place in the next few days.

- The Pay to the Order Of line provides a space for the name of the person or business to be paid. This person or business is entitled to make a claim against the check writer's checking account for the dollar amount stated on the check.

- The Pay to the Order Of line is followed by a box in which to write the amount of the check in numbers. Check writers should write the numbers as close as possible to the dollar sign so that no one can squeeze in additional numbers.

- The next line provides a space for the amount of the check in words. The amount written on this line must agree with the numeric entry. Check writers should draw a line after having written the amount. The line fills up the space so that no one can add more to the space.

- The lower portion of the check includes the name of the bank or financial institution in which the check writer's account is held. This is important when the check is presented for clearing purposes.

- The Memo line provides a space for the check writer to make a note as to the purpose of the

check. For instance, if the check is being written to a health care provider, this line can be used to write the person's account number. If the check is being written for a cousin's birthday, the check writer can include a birthday message. Never include a credit card account number, Social Security number, PIN, or other confidential information on this line.

- The Signature line follows the Memo line. The signature of the account holder shows that he or she wants the payment made from his or her checking account. It can be compared with a signature card held in the bank to verify that the account holder wrote the check.

- The first nine numbers at the bottom of the check are the "routing numbers," which provide information about the financial institution. The next numbers include an account number and a check number. These numbers are scanned when the check is processed to ensure accuracy.

12. Distribute a copy of **Exercise 8.2** from the *Student Workbook* to each student. Explain that this activity will provide practice in keeping a checkbook register. The balance at the end of the transaction list is $124.37. When the students complete the exercise, display **Visual 8.4** so that they can check their work. Make sure the students follow the rules for writing checks presented earlier.

13. Display **Visual 8.5**. Tell the students that Mr. Smith has a problem. Ask: Do you know what it means for a checking account to be "overdrawn"? **(Discuss the students' answers briefly. In discussion, establish the point that a checking account becomes overdrawn when the owner of the account writes checks for amounts greater than the amount of money available in his or her account. That is what Mr. Smith has done.)**

14. Explain that the bank may have paid Mr. Smith's checks even though he was overdrawn. However, that is unlikely. The more likely scenario is that the checks Mr. Smith wrote "bounced." Explain that a "bounced check," or an "overdraft," is a check written for an amount

greater than the amount of money in the check writer's account. Banks usually refuse to pay on an overdraft; instead, they "bounce" it back to the person who tried to cash it. An overdraft is often referred to in bank statements as an "NSF" (which stands for "non-sufficient funds"). Checking account holders should take care to avoid writing overdrafts. For one thing, overdrafts are expensive. The bank will charge a fee, as high as $35 or so, for each overdraft an account holder writes. The business to which an overdraft is written is also likely to charge a fee. Another very serious consequence is that a bounced check harms the check writer's reputation—in the eyes of the banker and the person to whom the check is written. While debit card transactions also withdraw money from checking accounts, as of 2010, the rules for overdraft are different for checks and debit cards; if a checking account does not have enough money for a transaction, a debit card purchase will be denied, unless the account holder has agreed to overdraft protection. In that case, the overdraft will be covered, but the account holder will pay an overdraft fee.

CLOSURE

Point out that people now handle many transactions without using cash—thanks to credit cards, debit cards, and various electronic innovations. Invite the students to speculate about whether a time will come when people stop using cash altogether. Explain that a cashless society has been predicted for a long time; however, most people still like to have a little cash in their pockets for emergencies or small purchases. What would it take to create a cashless society? What types of banking services would bring it to reality? *(The students may identify more widespread uses of ATMs, debit cards, direct deposit, automatic withdrawals, and online banking.)*

ASSESSMENT

Instruct the students to use the information they gathered on checking accounts in Procedure 4 of this lesson for this assignment. Tell them that they will act as public relations persons for a financial institution. Instruct them to write an advertisement about the institution's services. Their ads should include the institution's features, such as location and banking hours, and the features of the accounts offered, such as per-check fees, minimum balances, and so on. Distribute a copy of **Lesson 8 Assessment** from the *Student Workbook* to each student. The students may consult this assessment for ideas about the features and costs of checking accounts that might be included in their ads.

EXTENSION

Ask the students to go to www.bankrate.com and click on the "Check and Savings" tab. Here they will find a feature called "Find a Checking Account." Have them compare internet-based and local checking accounts to explore the similarities and differences between these types of accounts and ask them to report their findings in class.

Electronic Banking

Electronic banking may sound impersonal, but it's actually a fast and easy way to use banking services.

Electronic banking includes:

- Automated Teller Machines (ATMs)
- Debit cards
- Automatic withdrawals/transfers
- Direct deposits
- Online banking services

You can use an ATM to:

- make deposits
- make withdrawals (get cash)
- transfer money between accounts
- check your account balance

(Most debit cards can be used at the ATM)

You can use a debit card to:

- pay for purchases at the point of sale
- pay for purchases online

You can use a computer/smart phone to:

- check your account balance
- transfer money between accounts
- pay bills
- make payments on loans

FINANCIAL FITNESS FOR LIFE: Teacher Guide Grades 6-8
http://fffl.councilforeconed.org/6-8

Check Register

CHECK #	DATE	TRANSACTION DESCRIPTION	WITHDRAWAL/ TRANSACTIONS		√ T	FEE IF ANY	DEPOSIT/ ADDITIONS		BALANCE	
		Starting balance							$172	52

PLEASE BE SURE TO DEDUCT CHARGES THAT AFFECT YOUR ACCOUNT

Write a Check

Check Register Answer Sheet

CHECK #	DATE	TRANSACTION DESCRIPTION	WITHDRAWAL/ TRANSACTIONS		T	FEE IF ANY		DEPOSIT/ ADDITIONS		BALANCE	
		PLEASE BE SURE TO DEDUCT CHARGES THAT AFFECT YOUR ACCOUNT									
		Starting balance								$172	52
	9/4	album purchase	10	00						162	52
X	9/8	Deposit						83	46	245	98
	9/11	Grayson's Service Station	24	50						221	48
		oil change									
	9/15	Acme Jewelers	15	00						206	48
		deposit on class ring									
ATM	9/19	Cash withdrawal	40	00						166	48
X	9/22	Deposit						63	88	230	36
8455	9/23	Lee Johnson	5	00						225	36
		loan repayment									
8456	9/26	American Publishing	16	50						208	86
		subscription									
8457	9/27	Neighbor's Store	33	63						175	23
		mom's birthday gift									
X	9/29	Deposit						12	00	187	23
X	9/30	Automatic withdrawal	56	96						130	27
		auto loan									
auto	10/1	Service charge	5	90						124	37

A Hard Lesson for Mr. Smith

Banker:
Mr. Smith, your checking account is overdrawn.

Mr. Smith:
How can that be? I still have checks!

What Taxes Affect You?

LESSON DESCRIPTION AND BACKGROUND

This lesson focuses on taxes and the uses governments make of tax revenue. Tax revenue pays for public goods and services: roads, schools, court houses, police and fire protection, parks, national defense, and so on. Taxes are also used to fund transfer payments to people who receive Social Security, Medicare, disability, food stamp, and other benefits.

Public goods and services share two characteristics: non-exclusion and shared consumption. Non-exclusion refers to the impossibility of keeping people from using a public good. Everyone enjoys the benefits of living in a more secure country when national defense is provided to residents of a nation. For example, it would be impossible to exclude people from enjoying the benefits of a missile defense system simply because they didn't help pay for it. Shared consumption refers to the fact that one person's use of a public good or service does not stop other people from using it. If there is only one piece of pie at the dinner table and Grandpa eats it, others must go without pie. But one person's enjoyment of national security does not make it less available to others.

Students pay taxes in the form of sales taxes, and as they come into young-adulthood they will be obligated to pay income taxes. Most people will also pay property taxes and payroll taxes. And, of course, students use public goods and services. In this lesson, they learn about the link between the taxes they pay and the public goods and services they use.

Lesson 9 is correlated with national standards for mathematics and economics, and with personal finance guidelines, as shown in Tables 1-3 in the introductory section of this publication.

ECONOMIC AND PERSONAL FINANCE CONCEPTS

- Income tax
- Property tax
- Public goods and services
- Sales tax

OBJECTIVES

At the end of this lesson, the student will be able to:

- Define and explain **income tax**, **property tax**, and **sales tax**.
- Identify **goods** and **services** provided by government at the local, state, and federal levels.
- Explain why government provides some **goods** and **services**, but not others.

TIME REQUIRED

Two 45-minute class periods

MATERIALS

- A supply of sales receipts with sales tax included—enough for each student to have at least one (see **Procedure 6**)

- A transparency of **Visual 9.1**, **9.2**, **9.3**, **9.4**, **9.5**, and **9.6**

- A copy for each student of **Introduction** and **Vocabulary** sections of **Lesson 9** from the *Student Workbook*

- A copy for each student of **Reading 9.1** from the *Student Workbook*

- A copy for each student of **Lesson 9 Assessment** from the *Student Workbook*

ADDITIONAL RESOURCES

To download visuals, find related lessons, correlations to state standards, interactives, and more, visit http://fffl.councilforeconed.org/6-8/lesson9.

PROCEDURE

1. Introduce the lesson's focus on taxes. Define "taxes" as required payments of money to the government. Write the definition on the board.

2. Briefly describe a paradox. Governments use tax revenue to pay for things that many people want to have—schools and highways, for example. Yet many people complain about having to pay taxes. To illustrate, display **Visual 9.1**. Read through each statement and ask the students what the statements have in common. **(Each statement is a criticism of taxation.)**

3. To begin examining this paradox, point out that some complaints focus on a level of taxation ("My property tax is too high!"), while others are concerned with certain types of taxes ("There shouldn't be a sales tax on clothing"). Ask the students to read through the statements again to determine which ones focus on levels of taxation and which focus on types of taxes. **(All except for the statements by Goldwater and Einstein appear to focus on levels of taxation.)**

4. Assign the students to read the Introduction and Vocabulary sections for **Lesson 9** in the *Student Workbook*. When they have finished reading, explain that not everybody complains about taxes. Display **Visual 9.2**. (Allow this visual to remain on display for discussion in **Procedure 12**.) Engage the students in a discussion of the statements made by Madison and Holmes. They are very strong statements. Ask: Why might Madison and Holmes claim that taxation is "essential," and "the price we pay for civilization"? **(The goal here is not to focus in on a particular conclusion about this large and complex issue. It is merely to get the students started thinking about the relationship between tax revenue and the provision of public goods.)**

5. Ask the students what type of taxes they pay. **(The sales tax would be a tax they all pay unless their state doesn't have a sales tax).** Define sales tax as a tax consumers pay on many items they purchase.

6. Provide each student with one or more receipts for purchases made locally. Help the students locate the sales tax amount charged on the receipt. Explain that the sales tax is a percentage of the sale price. For instance, a city might have a four percent sales tax and the state in which that city is located might have a two percent sales tax. In that case, a consumer would pay six cents in sales taxes for every dollar he or she spent on consumer goods. Tell the students to look again at the receipts provided. In some cases, the sales tax percentage will be printed on the receipt. Call on students to report the percentage rates if the percentages are shown on these receipts. If the receipts do not indicate the percentage rate, ask the students to calculate that percentage. You may wish to note that many states exempt certain purchases (such as food or clothing) from sales taxation. The receipts you distribute may include some items for which sales taxes are paid and others that are exempt.

7. Explain that, in addition to sales tax, communities impose "property taxes." A property tax is a tax on real estate and, sometimes, on personal property such as cars and boats.

8. Some cities and most states impose "income taxes;" the federal government also imposes an income tax. An income tax is a tax based on taxpayers' incomes. Income tax rates go up as taxpayers' incomes go up.

9. Distribute a copy of **Reading 9.1** from the *Student Workbook* to each student. Ask the students to read the case it describes and to answer questions 1-3. Discuss their answers. **(1. Private funding of the road would be unlikely, since the project would most likely not be profitable for a private company; voluntary contributions would probably be insufficient, since not everybody would be willing to contribute. 2. If a new road does get built, it will**

probably be financed by tax revenue. 3. New roads in the students' community are financed by tax revenue.)

10. To elaborate on **Reading 9.1**, explain that road construction generally is a government project, financed by tax revenue. Some streets in local communities are constructed and maintained by the local government. Some larger roads are constructed and maintained by the county or state government. The federal government provides interstate highways.

11. Explain that roads are one example of government-provided goods and services. These are also called "public goods and services." Ask the students to identify other goods and services in their community, state, and country that are publicly owned and maintained. Record their answers on the board. *(Answers might include public libraries, parks, museums, public health clinics or hospitals, police and fire protection, schools, sewage system. The students are not likely to know which level of government provides particular goods and services.)*

12. Raise the question of why government provides some goods and services but not others. Why does the government provide highways but not restaurants or hardware stores? Explain that governments provide goods and services that are not likely to be provided in any other way. A private construction company would be unlikely to build a major highway, on its own, because it would have no good way to charge people for using the highway and, thus, no way to earn a profit from building it. Governments get the money to provide public goods and services by requiring citizens to pay taxes. Refer to **Visual 9.2**. Ask the students to think again about President Madison's and Oliver Wendell Holmes's statements in support of taxes. Ask them to explain Madison's and Holmes's statements in their own words. *(The students should recognize that taxes are essential to the provision of public goods and services.)*

13. Display **Visual 9.3**. Discuss the role of local governments in providing public services. Explain that items on this list are fairly typical of goods and services provided by local government, but the profile of services varies somewhat from place to place. Also, some services (public education, for example) receive funding from local, state, and federal governments. Ask the following questions:

a. What goods and services are provided within our school? *(Answers might include teachers, custodial workers, secretaries, counseling, books, computers, classrooms, lighting, heat, art supplies, etc.)*

b. What parks and recreational programs does our town, city, or county provide? *(Answers might include local parks, skating rinks, pools, ball fields, etc.)*

c. What resources do our law enforcement programs need to meet their responsibilities? *(Answers might include police officers, police cars, police bicycles or horses, courthouses, judges, court clerks, jails, guards, safety and educational programs, etc.)*

14. Display **Visual 9.4**. Discuss the role of state governments in providing public goods and services. Ask:

a. Is anyone acquainted with someone who is currently attending a state college or university? Who is it? Which state university or college does he or she attend? *(Answers will vary.)*

b. Does your acquaintance (or relative) have to pay any money to attend the state college or university? *(The students may or may not be aware that, in most cases, students at state colleges or universities are required to pay some portion of the cost of their education. Explain that the price the students pay at state schools is far lower than the actual cost of their education because the state pays for a portion of the total cost.)*

c. What state parks have you visited? **(Answers will vary.)** What types of services are provided *there*? **(Again, answers will vary, but many state parks offer camping grounds, picnic areas, covered shelters, security, and nature programs.)**

15. Display **Visual 9.5**. Discuss the role of the federal government in providing public goods and services and in making payments to individuals to help them through rough times. The latter payments are called "transfer payments." Ask:

a. What types of goods and services are included in our national defense system? **(Answers might include fighter jets, transport jets, helicopters, tanks, missiles, computers, submarines, aircraft carriers, salaries for military personnel including fighting forces, doctors and nurses, lawyers, translators, etc.)**

b. What programs help people through rough times, or are programs to which people are entitled? **(Housing programs, food stamps, Medicare, Medicaid, Social Security.)**

c. Why does the federal government offer these types of programs? **(Explain that one goal of federal policy, established by various acts of Congress, is to provide some measure of economic equity for citizens. This means that we, as a society, have decided that people should have some of their most important basic needs provided by government if they are having a hard time providing these things for themselves.)**

d. What is Social Security and Medicare? **(Social Security is a federal program to provide the elderly with retirement income; to assist minor children of a parent who has died; and to assist people living with disabilities. This program is not designed to cover all of the costs these people may incur; it is considered a supplement to the money people have saved for retirement, or to assist a family to cope with loss of income due to death or dis-**

ability. Medicare is a federal health care program for people 65 years of age and older.)

e. Which of these programs do you consider to be among the most important? **(Answers will vary. The students should recognize that we have all have benefited from national defense and interstate highways. The students may also know people who are receiving Social Security or have received housing assistance, food stamps, Medicaid assistance, or unemployment compensation.)**

16. Remind the students that they regularly pay sales taxes. However, in a few years, they will be paying income taxes. Income taxes are taxes on income, both earned income (salaries, wages, tips, commissions) and unearned income (interest from savings accounts or other investments, stock dividends, etc.).

a. Explain that when the students begin to work, their first official tax-related duty will be to fill out a Form W-4. This form will tell each worker's employer how much money he or she should withhold from the worker's paycheck for income tax. The withheld tax is based on an estimate of the income tax the worker will owe. The amount of tax owed will be based, in part, on how many people rely on the worker for their support. These people are the worker's "dependents." When a worker claims zero dependents, the employer will withhold the largest tax allowable. When a worker claims one dependent, the employer will withhold a smaller amount of money. You may not claim more than one dependent if you have no one financially dependent on you, other than yourself. And you may not claim yourself if your parents or guardians claim you as one of their dependents.

b. Point out that "withholding" is the money that is withheld from a paycheck, sent to the government, and credited to the employee's tax bill. This helps the employee "save" money for taxes. Explain that sometimes employees withhold a little more than is required. This practice assures an employee that his or her taxes will be covered for the year, and the extra money that is withheld will be returned in the form of a refund. On the other hand, withholding more than is required deprives the employee of money he or she could be spending or saving during the year and gives "Uncle Sam" an interest-free loan.

17. Display **Visual 9.6**. Explain that it often comes as a surprise to many new workers who get their first paychecks and discover they have not received all of the money they expected. These workers forgot, or never knew about, money that would be withheld from their paychecks for taxes. State and federal (and in some places, local) taxes pay for the goods and services already discussed. FICA, a payroll tax established by the Federal Insurance Contributions Act, pays into the funds established for Social Security and Medicare. These payroll taxes essentially provide transfer payments from those who are working (and contributing to this payroll tax) to those who are not currently working and have qualified to receive Social Security and Medicare.

CLOSURE

Use the following questions to review the lesson:

- What are taxes? *(Taxes are required payments of money to the government.)*

- What types of taxes do you pay currently? *(In some states, students pay sales taxes; some students may pay income taxes and payroll taxes.)*

- What are income taxes? *(Taxes paid on earned income and unearned income.)*

- What is earned income? *(Money received from salaries, wages, tips, commissions.)*

- What are some examples of unearned income? *(Dividends, interest, capital gains, etc.)*

- What goods and services do local taxes provide? *(Local roads, police, parks, and so on.)*

- What goods and services do state taxes provide? *(State roads, state parks, state courts, prisons, and so on.)*

- What goods and services do federal taxes provide? *(National defense, the space program, interstate highways, and so on.)*

- Why must governments provide these goods and services? *(Private industry is not likely to provide these goods and services because it is difficult to receive payment in return for their use.)*

ASSESSMENT

Distribute a copy of **Lesson 9 Assessment** from the *Student Workbook* to each student. Assign the students to read the information provided and answer Questions 1-4, working independently.

The answers are as follows: *1. Personal information (such as the employee's name and Social Security number) is reported, along with the number of dependents, to estimate the amount of withholding. 2. The students should respond with any of the goods and services provided by the state, such as state universities, highways and bridges, prisons, and so on. 3. The students should respond with the goods, services, and transfer payments provided by the federal government, such as national defense, transportation, energy programs, income support programs, and so on. 4. The money collected through FICA deductions goes toward the support of Social Security and Medicare. Federal income tax pays for other government-provided goods and services and transfer payments.*

EXTENSION

Explain that public schools are primarily funded by state and local taxes. When school districts have a need that is going to cost more than current tax revenue will meet, one option is to ask area residents to allow a tax increase. As a class, instruct students to brainstorm goods and services they would like their school to have available to them. Suggest goods and services that teachers would like to have available for students. Instruct each student to construct a table with four columns containing the following headings from left to right: Good/Service, Yes, No, Priority. Title the table, "Goods and Services to be Funded through a Tax Increase." They should record their list of goods and services in the Goods/Services column. This will serve as a survey form. Instruct them to use the form to survey their next-door neighbors. They should ask the neighbor if they would support a tax increase for each item and record the responses by checking the yes or no cell. For those goods or services the neighbor indicates as worthy of a tax increase, have the students ask the neighbor to prioritize the list, with 1 being the highest priority.

When surveys are complete, have the students tally responses on the board to ascertain which items were seen as priorities their neighbors would be willing to fund through increased taxes. Explain that local tax initiatives are proposed in a similar way. The school board decides on the priorities for the school district and asks residents to support those priorities by increased taxes. The residents can vote whether they will support the school board policies.

Tax Troubles

People who complain about taxes can be divided into two classes: men and women.

--Unknown

The hardest thing in the world to understand is the income tax.

--Albert Einstein

When there's a single thief, it's robbery. When there are a thousand thieves, it's taxation.

--Vanya Cohen

America is a land of taxation that was founded to avoid taxation.

--Laurence J. Peter

We must care for each other more, and tax each other less.

--Bill Archer

I shall never use profanity except in discussing house rent and taxes.

--Mark Twain

The income tax created more criminals than any other single act of government.

--Barry Goldwater

Another Point of View

The power of taxing people and their property is essential to the very existence of government.

--James Madison

Taxation is the price we pay for civilization.

--Oliver Wendell Holmes

Local Government (City, County, or Local districts) Provides...

- Local roads, signals, and signs

- Elementary and secondary schools (in part)

- Libraries

- Community parks

- Streetlights and sidewalks

- Police and fire protection

- City courts

- City jails

- Health clinics and hospitals (sometimes)

State Government Provides...

- State highways and bridges

- State colleges/universities

- Assistance with funding local schools

- State police and highway patrols

- State prisons

- State courts

- State parks

- Job training programs

FINANCIAL FITNESS FOR LIFE: Teacher Guide Grades 6-8
http://fffl.councilforeconed.org/6-8

Federal Government Provides...

Goods and Services

- National defense
- Veterans' programs
- Military and economic assistance to other countries
- Foreign embassies
- Agricultural programs
- Transportation
- Assistance to elementary and secondary schools
- Job training programs
- Financial assistance for college students
- The space program
- Energy programs
- Scientific research
- Prisons
- Federal law enforcement (the FBI)
- Tax collection
- National parks
- Federal Reserve System /Currency

Transfer Payments

- Food stamps
- Housing payments for the poor
- Social Security and Medicare
- Health care for the poor (Medicaid)

Who Got a Piece of My Paycheck?

You've landed your first job. The local convenience store will pay you $8.00 per hour. You have agreed to work 25 hours per week. Quick, do the math!

That was the good news. Now, here's the bad news. You, like every other worker, must have some of your money withheld to pay taxes. This is how it breaks down:

First week's wages: $200.00

Federal Tax Withheld (one exemption
claimed on Form W-4): $9.00

State Taxes (amount varies from state to state): 5.00

Social Security Tax Withheld:. 8.40

Medicare Tax:. 2.90

Total deductions: $25.30

Net Pay (what you take home):. $174.70

FINANCIAL FITNESS FOR LIFE: Teacher Guide Grades 6-8
http://fffl.councilforeconed.org/6-8

©Council for Economic Education

Why Save?

LESSON DESCRIPTION AND BACKGROUND

The students learn about saving and investing, and they consider the importance of setting short-term, medium-term, and long-term savings goals. They use math skills to solve problems and they play a game designed to emphasize the importance of setting goals and working toward a goal. Finally, they engage in a family activity that focuses on the opportunity cost of saving.

Lesson 10 is correlated with national standards for mathematics and economics, and with personal finance guidelines, as shown in Tables 1-3 in the introductory section of this publication.

ECONOMIC AND PERSONAL FINANCE CONCEPTS

- Investing
- Long-term goals
- Medium-term goals
- Opportunity cost
- Saving
- Scarcity
- Short-term goals

OBJECTIVES

At the end of this lesson, the student will be able to:

- Recognize the importance of setting goals.
- Define **short-term**, **medium-term**, and **long-term goals**.
- Use math to project **savings** goals.
- Identify the **opportunity cost** of **saving**.

TIME REQUIRED

Two 45-minute class periods

MATERIALS

- A transparency of **Visual 10.1** and **10.2**

- A copy of the **Introduction to Theme 4** and **Introduction** and **Vocabulary** sections of **Lesson 10** from the *Student Workbook*

- A copy of **Activity 10.1** for each group of four students

- A copy for each student of **Exercise 10.1** and **10.2** from the *Student Workbook*

- A copy for each student of **Lesson 10 Assessment** from the *Student Workbook*

- Scissors and a pair of dice for each group of four students

- Three 4" x 6" index cards for each student

- Sticky notes or index cards

ADDITIONAL RESOURCES

To download visuals, find related lessons, correlations to state standards, interactives, and more, visit http://fffl.councilforeconed.org/6-8/lesson10.

PROCEDURE

1. Introduce the lesson's focus on saving and goal setting. Explain that the act of setting a goal helps people to think clearly about the steps that might be needed to reach that goal. When we state clearly what we want to do, ideas about how to do it often come into focus. Distribute a copy of the **Introduction to Theme 4** and **Introduction** and **Vocabulary** sections of **Lesson 10** from the *Student Workbook* to each student. Ask the students to read these passages as a way to introduce the ideas found in this lesson.

2. Pose a hypothetical goal for the students to consider—e.g., getting elected president of the school's student council. (Note: Not all schools have student councils. Please substitute a different goal if this goal is unsuitable for your school.) Ask: what steps would you take in a campaign for the student council presidency? *(Discuss the students' responses briefly. Remind the students that some campaign activities take place months before the election, while others must be completed weeks or just days prior to the election. Continue the inquiry as described below.)*

a. Divide the class into small groups. Allow about 10 minutes for each group to brainstorm ideas about "Things to Do to Prepare for an Election Campaign," recording each idea on a sticky note or index card (one idea per note).

b. On the board, draw five large circles, labeling them, from left to right, "Three months before the election," "One month before the election," "Two weeks before the election," "One week before the election," "One day before the election."

c. Invite the students to post their notes on the board in the appropriate circles.

d. Discuss the students' responses. Focus the discussion on the reasoning behind the proposed steps.

3. Explain that, like campaigning for an office, saving money in order to achieve a goal also requires planning.

a. Check briefly to make sure the students know what saving money means. *(Putting money aside from current income so that it will be available for some use in the future—e.g., buying a car, paying college tuition, etc.)*

b. Explain an important first step: When people decide to save money, they need to decide where they will put the money they save. It is possible to put one's savings into a coffee can or a desk drawer at home, but most people would prefer to deposit their savings in an account at a bank or another financial institu-

tion. Why might people prefer to deposit their savings in an account? *(When people deposit savings in a bank account, their money earns interest. The money they save becomes a financial investment; it will grow; and the depositors will eventually have more dollars and cents than they originally deposited.)*

c. Pause to clarify and emphasize the underlying reason for saving. Ask:

i. Why do people take the trouble to save? *(Saving money positions people to do things in the future that they might otherwise not be able to do—to buy a car, make a down payment on a house, pay for a college education, make a charitable contribution, respond to an emergency without going broke, etc.)*

ii. Are you saving money for a goal of your own right now? *(Responses will vary.)*

4. Display **Visual 10. 1**. By reference to the Visual, introduce the concepts of "short-term," "medium-term," and "long-term goals."

a. Go over the definitions. Note that the time spans used in the definitions are somewhat arbitrary, but they represent common-sense boundaries for these saving terms.

b. Ask the students to suggest goals (buying certain goods or services, for example) that might require short-, medium-, or long-term savings plans. *(Answers might include saving money to attend a sporting event or to go to the movies [short-term goals]; saving money for an upcoming vacation [a medium-term goal]; saving money to buy a car or pay for a college education [long-term goals].)*

c. Suppose that the goal is to save $600 to buy a new computer. Could this be a short-term goal for one saver and a long-term goal for another saver? Explain. *(The amount that can be saved in any time period varies depending upon an individual's earnings and expenses. If Samantha earns a good salary and doesn't have many expenses, she might be able to save $600 in a short time; if Albert* *earns the minimum wage and has many expenses, he might need a long time to save $600.*)

5. Display **Visual 10.2**. Explain the relationship between short-term and long-term goals.

• Long-term goals are usually more difficult to reach than short-term goals. When a person tries to save money over, say, four years, the plan might be difficult to follow for many reasons. Emergencies might pop up, causing the saver to spend money he hadn't planned to spend. Or the saver might get a new idea about what it would be really important for him to do with his money now, rather than sticking to his savings plan. If the emergency creates an urgent need, or the new idea looks more attractive than the original savings goal, the goal may be abandoned in favor of the alternative. In economic terms, the "opportunity cost" of saving in these cases—not being able to cope with the emergency, not pursuing the new idea—might seem to be too high. (As necessary, review the definition of "opportunity cost" as the next-best alternative given up when a choice is made.)

• One way of coping with the difficulty of saving for long-term goals is to break them down by setting a sequence of short-term goals that will lead, eventually, to reaching the long-term goal. The one-step-at-a-time approach can give savers a feeling of accomplishment that motivates them to keep going.

6. Distribute a copy of **Exercise 10.1** from the *Student Workbook* to each student. Go over the directions. Assign the students to read the three cases and answer the questions posed at the end of each case, working independently. Discuss the students' answers.

Answers to Exercise 10.1:

1. It will take Jose 25 weeks, or a little more than 6 months, to save enough for the bracelet. This is a medium-term goal. Explanation: Jose earns $43 a week; he saves $18 for college and spends $15. That leaves $10

every week to save for the bracelet. ($43-$18-$15=$10.) The bracelet costs $250. $250/$10 = 25 weeks to save. 25 weeks divided by approximately 4 weeks in a month equals 6.25 months. If Jose saves his money in an interest-bearing bank account, he will meet his goal earlier.

2. It will take Lauren just over 8 weeks to save for the saxophone. This is on the dividing line between a short- and medium-term goal. Explanation: Lauren saves $6 of her allowance money for college. That leaves $26 every week ($20 from babysitting and $6 from her allowance) to be saved for the saxophone. The saxophone costs $210. $210/$26 = 8.07 weeks, approximately 2 months.

3. Darnell will not be able to save enough money for his short-term goal. He earns $90 per week, saves $24, gives $5 to charity, and spends $10. This means he has $51 per week ($90 - $24 - $5 - $10 = $51) for the golf lessons. In six weeks Darnell will have only $306 ($51 x 6). He needs $54 more for the golf lessons. Answers will vary as to how Darnell could change his savings or spending plan in order to meet his goal.

7. Review the problems in **Exercise 10.1**, asking the students to identify, in each case, the opportunity cost of saving. *(When José, Lauren, and Darnell decided to save for the future, they gave up the chance to spend a certain amount of money in the present.)*

8. Introduce Rolling for a Goal, an activity designed to reinforce concepts related to savings goals.

a. Before starting the activity, copy enough sets of game cards from **Activity 10.1** to give each group of four a full set of cards. Divide the class into groups of four. Give a set of game cards and two dice to each group.

b. Give each student a copy of **Exercise 10.2** from the *Student Workbook*. Go over the directions; as necessary, help the students get started. Then have the students play the game.

c. When the students have finished the game, engage them in a discussion of differences among short-, medium-, and long-term savings goals. *(The students should recognize that achieving short-, medium-, or long-term goals depends on the amount of money saved each month and the number of months you will be able to save.)*

d. Ask the students if leaving a savings plan to chance (here, the roll of the dice) is a good idea. *(The students should recognize that many of the goals were not met when they did not save enough each month, or did not save long enough—factors that were determined by the roll of the dice.)*

CLOSURE

Distribute three 4" x 6" index cards to each student.

Have the students make up three story problems (similar to the problems in **Exercise 10.1**) about short-, medium-, and long-term savings goals. The students should write one problem on each card, with the answers on the back.

When the students have completed the task, put the cards in a box so the students can challenge one another.

ASSESSMENT

Distribute a copy of **Lesson 10 Assessment** from the *Student Workbook* to each student. Assign them to do the assessment, working independently. See **Visual 10.3** for an answer key to the assessment.

EXTENSION

Ask students to recall an item they wanted to buy in the Rolling for a Goal activity. Imagine that the outcome for each of them was that the item was a long-term goal. Explain that long-term goals can be converted to medium-term goals under certain conditions. An increase in income can change long-term goals into medium-term goals and medium-term goals

into short-term goals. Another way to reduce the time it takes to save for a goal is to give up other goods and services and save more money toward the goal. A third method is to seek a lower price for the good or service that is the goal. This could include finding the item on sale, buying last year's model, or finding a model that has fewer features.

Instruct students to use the Internet to identify similar items at lower prices. For example, they can visit websites such as Travelocity or Priceline for Disney vacations or visit eBay for a used mountain bike.

Short-term, Medium-term, and Long-term Goals

Short-term goals can be achieved in fewer than two months.

Medium-term goals may take from two months to three years to achieve.

Long-term goals require three or more years to achieve.

Long-term goals may be built upon short-term goals.

What Is the Relationship Between Long-term and Short-term Goals?

There is a relationship between long-term goals and short-term goals. Often, achieving a long-term goal requires reaching a set of short-term goals.

For example, in order to buy a $960 mountain bike in four years, Miranda needs to save $240 in each of the next four years, or $20 each month. The short-term savings target amounts to less than $1 per day.

Breaking long-term goals into medium- and short-term goals helps to make them seem achievable.

FINANCIAL FITNESS FOR LIFE: Teacher Guide Grades 6-8
http://fffl.councilforeconed.org/6-8

Lesson 10 Assessment: Answer Key

SHORT-, MEDIUM-, AND LONG-TERM GOALS

Use **Lesson 10 Assessment** to determine whether the students have mastered the concepts in this lesson. Answers are provided in the chart below.

Person	Amount to Be Saved	Amount Saved Each Month	How Many Months	How Many Years	Short- Medium- or Long-term
Abby	$780.00	$20.00	39	3.25	L
Ben	$25.00	$15.00	1.67	.14	S
Cherise	$700.00	$35.00	20	1.67	M
Danuka	$800.00	$70.00	11.43	.95	M
Emilio	$90.00	$50.00	1.8	.15	S
Festis	$2,900.00	$75.00	38.67	3.22	L

(It will take Cherise 20 months to reach her savings goal of $700.

The opportunity cost of saving for the future is the chance to spend money in the present. Accept any reasonable answer for each month's opportunity cost.

Examples: January opportunity cost = noisemakers and party hats for New Year's Party; February opportunity cost = red sweater for Valentine's Day; June opportunity cost = beverages and snacks for end-of-the-school-year picnic; July opportunity cost = flags, hot dogs, and apple pie for July Fourth celebration; September opportunity cost = pens, rulers and notebooks for back-to-school; October opportunity cost = pumpkins and costume for Halloween party; December opportunity cost = woolen hat and gloves for ski trip.)

Game Cards: Rolling for a Goal

These are the saving goals for **Exercise 10.2**, Rolling for a Goal.

Photocopy this page and cut out the cards to make one set of cards for each group of four students. Shuffle the cards and place them face down in a pile in front of the players in each group.

Mountain bike $1,099	Family trip to Disney World $3,200
New computer system $1,500	Clothing shopping spree $800
New mp3 player and docking station $500	Annual family membership in health club $1,600
One casual clothing outfit $180	Smart Phone and annual calling costs $1,200
Inline skates $270	Big screen TV for your bedroom $2,300
Album downloads for one year $240	Saddle and tack for horse $1,700
New furniture for your room $2,500	Two tickets to a professional basketball game $244
Drum set $2,700	Aquarium and fish $200
Spending money for class trip $300	Leather jacket $700
Snowboard and boots $500	Dance lessons for one year $630
Tennis lessons from a pro for one year $2,600	
Airfare to visit grandparents $1,000	

FINANCIAL FITNESS FOR LIFE: Teacher Guide Grades 6-8
http://fffl.councilforeconed.org/6-8

Let Lenders and Borrowers Be

LESSON DESCRIPTION AND BACKGROUND

The students learn how financial intermediaries foster exchanges between savers and borrowers. They learn how savers and borrowers benefit from these exchanges; they also learn about the opportunity costs of saving and borrowing.

Financial intermediaries perform an important function in our economy. In accepting deposits from savers and in lending money to borrowers, they support people in their efforts to reach their goals.

Lesson 11 is correlated with national standards for mathematics and economics, and with personal finance guidelines, as shown in Tables 1-3 in the introductory section of this publication.

ECONOMIC AND PERSONAL FINANCE CONCEPTS

- Demand
- Financial intermediaries
- Interest
- Opportunity cost
- Profit
- Revenue
- Supply

OBJECTIVES

At the end of this lesson, the student will be able to:

- Define **interest**.
- Explain that **interest** rates are determined by **supply** and **demand**.
- Identify the **opportunity cost** incurred by savers and borrowers.

TIME REQUIRED

One or two 45-minute class periods

MATERIALS

- A copy for each student of **Introduction** and **Vocabulary** sections of **Lesson 11** from the *Student Workbook*

- A transparency of **Visual 11.1**

- A copy for each student of **Exercise 11.1** from the *Student Workbook*

- A copy for each student of **Lesson 11 Assessment** from the *Student Workbook*

ADDITIONAL RESOURCES

To download visuals, find related lessons, correlations to state standards, interactives, and more, visit http://fffl.councilforeconed.org/6-8/lesson11.

PROCEDURE

1. Introduce the lesson's focus on "financial intermediaries"—banks, savings and loan associations, and credit unions. Explain that these institutions are intermediaries because they bring savers and borrowers together. They offer savings accounts in which people can deposit money and earn interest. They offer loans for people who want to borrow money. Money deposited by savers provides money that can be lent to borrowers. Distribute a copy of **Introduction** and **Vocabulary** sections of **Lesson 11** from the *Student Workbook* to each student. Use the passages in this handout to reinforce the important role of financial intermediaries.

2. Display **Visual 11.1**. Use the visual to illustrate the role of the bank in bringing savers and borrowers together. Draw attention to the smiling faces shown in the visual. Ask:

a. Why are the savers and the borrowers represented by smiling faces? *(**The savers smile because their money will be safe, and they will earn interest on it. The borrowers smile because the loans they obtain will enable them to do things—buy a car or a house, e.g.—that they otherwise could not afford to do.**)*

b. The answers to the smiley-face question emphasize benefits for savers and borrowers. Is that all there is to it? Is there any cost that comes with saving? With borrowing? *(**Savers and borrowers experience opportunity cost. For savers, the opportunity cost is the next-best use they could have made of their money if they had not deposited it in a savings account. For borrowers, it is the next-best use they could have made of their money in the future if they had not obligated themselves to follow a repayment schedule into the future.**)*

3. Challenge the students to think about the interest payments banks pay to savers. Ask: Why wouldn't banks decide to lower expenses simply by paying really low interest rates? *(**The interest paid to savings account holders must exceed the next-best alternative they have for saving. For example, if Bank A decided to lower expenses by paying a far lower rate of interest than Bank B paid, many depositors would move their savings to Bank B. Bank A then would have to adjust its rates or risk losing its depositors.**)*

4. Explain that banks are businesses, like grocery stores or software manufacturers. Bank owners are in business to make a profit. "Profit" is the money bank owners have left after they have paid their "operating costs." The operating costs include the cost of employees' wages, rent for office space, utilities, equipment, etc. Another cost is the interest payments banks

make to their depositors. Money to pay operating costs comes from the bank's "revenue." Most bank revenue comes from interest paid by borrowers. Profits or losses are the difference between revenues and expenses.

5. Review the concept of financial intermediaries by suggesting a further comparison between banks and other businesses—supermarkets, for example. Financial institutions and supermarkets are places where people engage in "exchanges." For example: a milk producer wants to sell milk; a consumer wants to buy milk. The supermarket provides a place where that exchange between producer and consumer can occur. Similarly: a saver wants to put money in a safe place and earn interest on it; a borrower wants to borrow money, and is willing to pay interest to do so. A financial institution provides a place where that exchange between saver and borrower can occur. As is the case in other markets, the "prices" (interest rates) charged in these exchanges are established through the interaction of buyers and sellers. Tell the class that the next activity shows how that interaction occurs.

6. Distribute to each student a copy of **Exercise 11.1** from the *Student Workbook*. Tell the students to read the story and answer Questions 1-5 in writing. After the students have written their answers, discuss their work as follows. *(**1. The demand for milk increased when people's taste for milk increased. One factor that can affect the demand for a product is a change in people's tastes and preferences. 2. The quantity of milk supplied stayed the same. The cows in the area could produce only so much milk, and there wasn't enough time for farmers to adjust the size of their herds. 3. The price of milk went up because demand increased while supply stayed constant. 4. The price of bananas and pineapple juice most likely increased too. They were complements to the milk, meaning they were items that people bought along with the milk. When the demand for an item goes up, the demand for its complement also goes up. When the**

demand for milk increased, the demand for bananas and pineapple juice would also have increased. Therefore, the price of bananas and pineapple juice would have increased. 5. The farmers in Cow Town would have liked to increase their milk production in order to benefit as much as possible from the new, high prices for milk. However, it would be difficult for them to increase milk production without getting more cows, and that would take time.)

7. Explain that the "supply" of and "demand" for money passing through financial intermediaries determines the "interest rate", which is the price of money. This is similar to the way in which the supply of and demand for milk passing through the grocery store in Cow Town determines the price of milk. (Note to the teacher: This lesson provides an opportunity for you to develop a supply and demand model for your more advanced students.)

8. Explain that "savers," who are the suppliers of funds, will be willing to save more money at higher interest rates and less money at lower interest rates. Remind the students that this is similar to the case of the farmers who would be willing to supply more milk at higher prices and less milk at lower prices. The farmers would take money they had budgeted for savings, or for spending on other items needed for the farm, and spend it to buy more cows. The "opportunity cost" would be the next-best use of the farmers' money. In the same way, savers have other uses for their money. The interest rate offered by a financial institution must be high enough to encourage savers to save their money instead of spending it. The higher the interest rate, the more people will save; the lower the interest rate, the less they will save.

9. Point out that "borrowers", on the other hand, are the demanders of funds. They will borrow less money at higher interest rates and more money at lower interest rates. Borrowers also have an opportunity cost. The higher the interest rate, the more they will have to give up because of higher loan repayment costs.

10. Explain that, in general, the rate of interest paid to savers and paid by borrowers is determined in the marketplace by supply and demand. What savers provide in savings and what borrowers buy in the way of loans relates to how they view the opportunity cost of saving and borrowing at different prices (interest rates).

CLOSURE

Use the following questions to review the lesson.

- What are financial intermediaries? *(Institutions that bring savers and borrowers together, transferring funds from those who have them to those who want them.)*

- What are some examples of financial intermediaries? *(Banks, credit unions, savings and loan associations.)*

- What is the price paid to savers for saving or paid by borrowers for borrowing? *(Interest.)*

- How is the rate of interest determined? *(By supply and demand.)*

- Why would savers want to be a part of the banking process? *(Savers get a safe place to deposit their savings; they also earn interest on their deposits.)*

- Why would borrowers want to be a part of this process? *(Borrowers can get money to use now; they can pay the money back over time.)*

- Why would banks want to be a part of this process? *(Banks earn income by facilitating exchange among those who wish to save and those who wish to borrow. Banks profit by making wise loans with their deposits.)*

- Why are interest rates higher for borrowers than for savers? *(The interest rate banks charge to borrowers must be sufficient to cover their operating costs and their interest payments to savers, and to provide a profit to bank owners.)*

- What might happen if borrowers failed to repay debts and interest? **(The bank would not be able to cover its costs, and it might fail.)**

ASSESSMENT

Distribute to each student a copy of **Lesson 11 Assessment** from the *Student Workbook*. Assign the students to do the assessment, working independently. **(Answers: 1.C; 2. B; 3. F; 4. A; 5.E ; 6.D.)**

EXTENSION

The interaction of supply and demand plays an important role in establishing interest rates as well as the prices of resources and consumer goods and services. Continue instruction on how an equilibrium price is established by presenting the lesson, *The Prices are Changing*, from EconEdLink, located at http://www.econedlink.org/e747.

Everybody's Bank

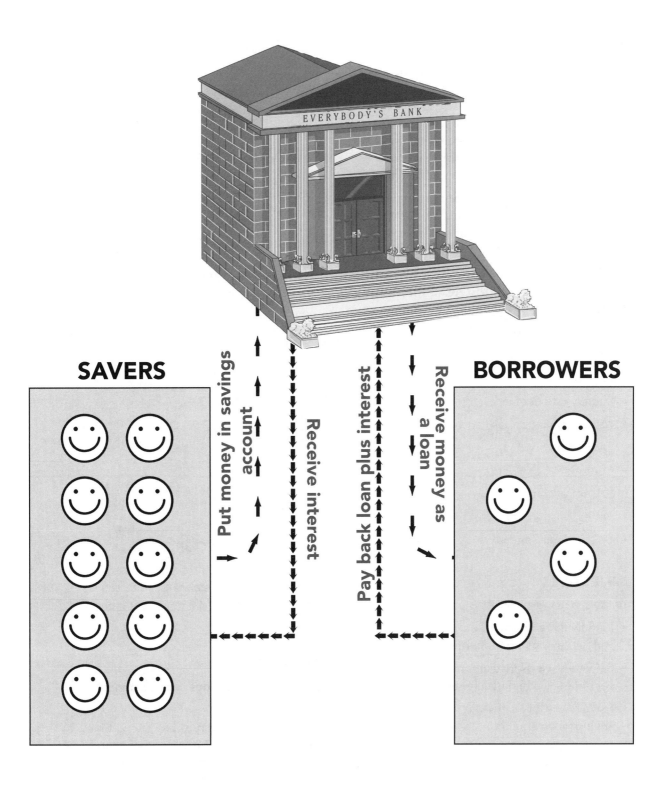

Types of Savings Plans and Investments

LESSON DESCRIPTION AND BACKGROUND

The students learn about various types of government-insured savings instruments, noting the advantages and disadvantages of each. They learn that savings and investment instruments carry various types of risk, including inflation risk, interest rate risk, and financial risk. They also learn that risk must be measured against reward.

Lesson 12 is correlated with national standards for mathematics and economics, and with personal finance guidelines, as shown in Tables 1-3 in the introductory section of this publication.

ECONOMIC AND PERSONAL FINANCE CONCEPTS

- Certificate of deposit (CD)
- Financial risk
- Inflation risk
- Interest rate risk
- Money market deposit account
- Opportunity cost
- Portfolio
- Savings account
- Savings instrument
- U.S. Savings Bond

OBJECTIVES

At the end of this lesson, the student will be able to:

- Identify the advantages and disadvantages of various **savings instruments**.
- Select a **savings instrument** suited to a given set of needs at a particular time.
- Explain why it is important to shop around for **savings instruments**.
- Identify types of **risk** associated with various savings plans and investments.
- Identify and explain the **opportunity cost** associated with saving and investing.

TIME REQUIRED

Three 45-minute class periods

MATERIALS

- A copy for each student of **Introduction** and **Vocabulary** sections of **Lesson 12** from the *Student Workbook*
- A transparency of **Visual 12.1**
- A copy for each student of **Exercise 12.1**, **12.2**, **12.3**, and **12.4** from the *Student Workbook*
- 103 pennies
- Calculators (one for each student)
- Newspaper photos or advertising pictures of items such as television sets, DVD players, car stereo systems, clothing items, computer equipment
- A copy for each student of **Lesson 12 Assessment** from the *Student Workbook*

ADDITIONAL RESOURCES

To download visuals, find related lessons, correlations to state standards, interactives, and more, visit http://fffl.councilforeconed.org/6-8/lesson12.

PROCEDURE

Part 1: Types of Savings and Investment Instruments

1. Introduce the lesson by explaining that a "savings instrument" is a tool that enables people to save their money for future uses. People often save money to make small and large purchases in the future—for example, an appliance,

a television set, a house, a car, or college education for the kids. They also save for emergencies or to have a source of income during retirement. Distribute a copy of **Introduction** and **Vocabulary** sections of Lesson 12 fom the *Student Workbook* to each student. Tell the students that this lesson will introduce them to different types of savings instruments and the risks that investors take in holding these instruments.

2. Introduce the concept of risk. "Risk" refers to the possibility of loss. In most banks, the possibility of loss is reduced or eliminated by insurance that guarantees the safety of depositors' money in different savings instruments. Where this insurance applies, you cannot lose your deposit, even if the bank goes out of business. The Federal Deposit Insurance Corporation (FDIC) currently insures deposits up to $250,000 in a bank that displays its logo. The National Credit Union Association (NCUA) does the same for credit unions.

3. Explain that there are many ways to save. The variety in types of savings instruments can make choosing the best method very confusing. In fact, there is no one best method. Individuals have different incomes, different savings goals, and different time lines for meeting their goals. Individuals thus need to familiarize themselves with the various plans and choose one or more that will best meet their needs.

4. Define "portfolio" as a person's financial security "package" or collection. Point out that this package or portfolio should include a variety of savings and investment instruments. In other words, it should be "diversified."

5. Explain that this lesson focuses on traditional savings instruments. Other lessons will address other instruments, including stocks, corporate bonds, and mutual funds. Each savings and investment instrument has advantages and disadvantages.

6. Explain that savings instruments provide funds for emergencies and for making purchases in the not-too-distant future. To minimize the risk of loss, accounts that are liquid and

insured are used for savings. (A "liquid" account is one from which you can withdraw money easily—e.g., a statement savings account.) Investments are used for long-term goals and to increase net worth. Investing involves risk. When you invest, you could lose part or all of your original investment, but you also have an opportunity to earn a greater return. There is a relationship between risk and return. The risk of an investment is related to its expected return. If you want higher returns, you must be willing to accept higher risk.

7. Ask the students to name all the saving or investment methods they've heard of, and list the ones they mention on the board. Circle those that are commonly offered by banks, savings and loan associations, and credit unions. These would include the savings account, the certificate of deposit, and the money market deposit account. These are the tools people can use to save money; in other words, these are savings instruments.

8. Distribute to each student a copy of **Exercise 12.1** from the *Student Workbook*. Have the students read the information it presents. Discuss the definitions as well as the advantages and disadvantages of each type of saving instrument. Then have the students answer the six questions posed at the end of the exercise. *(Answers: 1. In a statement savings account; 2. in a CD with duration of less than three years, or a money market deposit account, or a statement savings account; 3. in a money market deposit account, if you can keep your balance above the required amount, or in a statement savings account; 4. in a money market deposit account or a statement savings account; 5. in a CD; 6. in U.S. Savings Bonds.)*

9. Review the point that every savings decision has an opportunity cost. "Opportunity cost" is the next-best alternative given up when a choice is made. The person who decides to save gives up the next-best use she or he could have made with that money now.

10. Instruct the students to think about the types of saving methods introduced thus far and answer the following questions:

- If a person saves $1,000, what is the opportunity cost? *(It is what the saver could otherwise have done with that $1,000.)*

- If a person saves $1,000 in a Series EE Savings Bond rather than a statement savings account, what is the opportunity cost? *(It is access to the money for a period of time without penalty [loss of interest].)*

- If a person decides to save $1,000 in a 12-month CD rather than in a statement savings account, what is the opportunity cost? *(It is access to the money without penalty during the 12 months.)*

- If that person decides to save $1,000 in a regular savings account rather than in a CD, what is the opportunity cost? *(It is the higher interest rate he or she would have earned by placing the savings in a CD.)*

11. Explain that savings plans can vary quite a bit from one financial institution to another.

a. Distribute a copy of **Exercise 12.2** from the *Student Workbook* to each student. Assign the students to work in groups to visit local banks, savings and loans, or credit unions to obtain information about savings plans at each institution. In addition, have them compare information about accounts they find locally to accounts offered by some online banks.

b. Have the students record their findings on **Exercise 12.2**.

c. Ask the students, by groups, to present their findings to the class; consolidate those findings on an overhead transparency or Power Point slide.

d. Discuss the similarities and differences the students find among banks, savings and loans, and credit unions. Which institution had the best rates of interest for savers? Were penalties the same in all institutions?

CLOSURE

Use the following questions to review the lesson.

- What are some of the advantages of a money market deposit account? *(The saver usually can write checks on the account; the account is insured up to $250,000; the interest rate increases as market interest rates increase.)*

- What are some of the disadvantages of a money market deposit account? *(The saver must maintain a substantial minimum balance. The interest rate may be lower than the rate for CDs.)*

- What are some of the advantages of a statement savings account? *(The saver can withdraw the money as needed; the interest rate increases as market rates increase; the saver can maintain small balances.)*

- What are some of the disadvantages of a statement savings account? *(Statement savings accounts usually pay a lower interest rate than other options. Rates will decrease as market interest rates decrease.)*

- What are some of the advantages of a certificate of deposit? *(CDs pay a higher interest rate than regular savings accounts; the interest rate is "locked in," so if market interest rates go down, the saver continues to get the higher rate until the CD expires.)*

- What are the disadvantages of a certificate of deposit? *(The saver cannot withdraw money from a CD without significant penalty until the CD has expired; the interest rate is locked in so that if market interest rates go up, the CD holder is stuck with the lower interest rate.)*

- What are the advantages of U.S. Savings Bonds? *(Small amounts of money can be saved with U.S. Savings Bonds; the U.S. government guarantees them; they usually pay a higher rate of interest than regular savings accounts; possible tax advantages.)*

- What are the disadvantages of U.S. Savings Bonds? *(There is a penalty [loss of some interest] if they are cashed during the first five years. Series EE bonds issued on or after May 1, 2005, have a fixed rate of interest, meaning interest earned on existing bonds will not increase if general interest rates rise.)*

ASSESSMENT

Distribute to each student a copy of **Part 1: Types of Savings Plans** of **Lesson 12 Assessment** from the *Student Workbook*. Have the students do the assessment, working independently. *(Answers: 1. A; 2. D; 3. A or C, as long as the balance continues to meet the minimum required; 4. B; 5. A or C.)*

Part 2: Saving and Investing Are Risky Business

1. Introduce Part 2 by noting that some people use savings accounts because they believe that savings accounts are risk-free. Explain that most banks and savings and loan associations carry insurance on their savings accounts through the Federal Deposit Insurance Corporation (FDIC). The FDIC currently insures an individual's accounts in one institution up to $250,000. In other words, if the bank or savings and loan closes and it is insured (nearly all of them are insured), the depositors will get all their money back from the FDIC if they have $250,000 or less deposited in that bank. The same type of insurance is available from the National Credit Union Association (NCUA) for credit unions. In addition, the federal government is the issuer of U.S. Savings Bonds, which effectively guarantees their repayment.

2. Explain that, for these reasons, the amount of the principal on deposit is secure with these savings plans. "Principal" is the amount of money placed in the account by the saver. Savers using these accounts do not risk losing their savings; however, they do face other risks that are important to understand.

3. Explain that one of these risks is "inflation risk." Hold off, for the moment, on defining this concept. To establish a basis for the students' understanding of inflation risk, conduct the following activity.

a. Invite a volunteer to the front of the class. Give the volunteer 100 pennies and explain that each penny represents $10. Ask the class: how much money does the volunteer have? *($1,000.)*

b. Explain to the volunteer that she could pay for a long-weekend holiday for $1,000, but she has decided to wait until next year to purchase a computer. She places the money in a regular savings account. Even though the interest rate on a regular savings account can fluctuate over time, explain that in this case the interest rate did not change throughout the year, and the volunteer earned interest at a rate of three percent on the $1,000. Ask: how much money does the volunteer have in her account after one year? *($1,030.)*

You may have to review how interest is figured. The formula is:

Interest Earned = Principal x Interest Rate x Time

(Based on one year, with annual interest compounding; interest rate is expressed as a decimal in this calculation.)

c. Give the volunteer three more pennies.

d. Display **Visual 12.1**. Focus now on the concept of "inflation risk" as defined on the visual. This is the risk that the value of one's investments will not increase as rapidly as the rate of inflation. "Inflation" is a general rise in prices. During a time of inflation, not all prices increase; but prices on average do increase. When prices increase, your money is worth less and you lose buying power.

e. To provide an example, explain to the class that the rate of inflation for the year was four percent. If the price of the computer increased at the rate of inflation, the price of the computer after a year will be $1,040 (1.04 x $1,000). Ask the class if the volunteer has enough money to buy the computer now. *(No. The saver is worse off now because she has lost purchasing power over the year.)* The student was guaranteed that she would not lose any of the money placed in the savings account, and that she would earn interest. But, given the four percent rate of inflation, the interest she earned was not sufficient to maintain the purchasing power of her money. Have the student return to her seat.

4. Distribute to each student a copy of **Exercise 12.3** from the *Student Workbook*. If possible, display pictures, cut from newspaper or magazine ads, of the five items listed on the exercise. Go over the directions as necessary. Then have the students calculate the percentage change in the price of each item and answer questions 1-5. The percentage-change answers are listed in the table below. The amount in the account at the end of the year is $1,004.25. The answers to the questions follow:

1. **The computer and the camcorder.**

2. **None.**

3. **One year's wardrobe.**

4. **The plain television set.**

5. **For the car stereo system and one year's wardrobe.**

5. Direct the students back to the description of certificates of deposits in **Exercise 12.1** in the *Student Workbook*. Explain that certificates of deposit (CDs) offer a higher interest rate than a statement savings account and a guarantee that the interest rate will stay the same throughout the period in which the saver owns the CD. Suppose

someone purchases a CD for $2,070, and that it pays six percent interest annually but must be held by the saver for two years. Ask the class to calculate the amount of interest the saver will get over two years. Explain that in this case, the bank will compound the interest annually, meaning it will award interest at the end of year one and then again at the end of year two. *($2,070 x 1.06 = $2,194.20 after year one; $2,194.20 x 1.06 = $2,325.85 after year two).*

6. Instruct the class to calculate how much the plasma television set, the price of which is $2,070 this year, would cost after two years at an annual inflation rate of four percent the first year and seven percent the second year. Assume the television set increases in price at the same rate as inflation. *($2,070 x 1.04 = $2,152.80 after year one; $2,152.80 x 1.07 = $2,303.50 after year two).* Ask if the saver would have enough money to buy the television set if the money were kept in a CD. *(Yes.)* Explain that, even though the rate of inflation was higher than the interest rate in year two, the saver retained more purchasing power because he gained at a rate that was significantly higher than the inflation rate the first year. In this case, the purchasing power was mantained, but the savings gained very little new purchasing power.

7. Referring again to **Visual 12.1**, introduce a second type of risk. "Interest rate risk" is the risk that interest rates may change while the saver is "locked in" to a time deposit. To be locked in can be good for the saver if interest rates go down. But if interest rates go up, the saver will not earn the additional interest he or she could have earned if the rate had not been fixed.

Answers to Exercise 12.3

Item	Last year's price	This year's price	% change
computer	$997.00	$897.30	-10%
digital camcorder	$1,005.00	$954.75	-5%
plasma flat-panel TV	$3,000.00	$2,070.00	-31%
car stereo system	$995.00	$1,074.60	+8%
one year's wardrobe	$995.00	$1,094.50	+10%

8. Indicate that, in general, as inflation increases, interest rates increase. Notice in the last example that there was a four percent inflation rate one year and a seven percent inflation rate the next year. During the first year, the CD paid a rate higher than the inflation rate; in fact, it paid six percent. But during the last year, it did not keep up with inflation because it was locked in at a lower rate. Probably new CDs issued during that second year were yielding more than seven percent. So, during the last year, the money was not earning as much as it could have because it was tied up in a savings plan where it could not be removed without penalty.

9. Refer again to **Exercise 12.1** from the *Student Workbook*. Use the exercise to review the statement savings account, the money market deposit account, and U. S. Savings Bonds. Point out that the interest rate for the money market deposit account is flexible, as are the interest rates for Series I U.S. Savings Bonds and for statement savings accounts. This is particularly advantageous in an inflationary time. As interest rates spiral upward in the market, these savings instruments also pay a higher rate.

10. For a summary exercise on the lesson to this point, distribute a copy of **Exercise 12.4** from the *Student Workbook* to each student . Ask the students what they would do in the stated situations.

Answers to Exercise 12.4:

a. *A statement savings account would be the best choice; the fact that interest rates may be decreasing is immaterial in this situation since you want the money readily available, and there is not enough money to open a CD or a money market deposit account.*

b. *A money market deposit account or a statement savings account would be the best choice. You have enough savings to open a money market deposit account. You want to take advantage of the increasing rates.*

c. *A certificate of deposit of less than three years would be the best choice because*

you want to lock in the higher rate. You have enough savings to buy a CD.

d. *A Series I U.S. Savings Bond would be the best choice; you have a small amount of money, so CDs and the money market are not available to you; savings bonds generally pay a better rate than statement savings accounts. They can also have a tax advantage, especially if used for education.*

e. *A money market deposit account or a statement savings account would be the best choice if the periodic withdrawals are unpredictable.)*

11. To introduce a third type of risk, ask if anyone in the class has heard of the Great Depression. As necessary, explain briefly that the Great Depression was a deep and widespread downturn in the economy in the United States and elsewhere during the 1930s. Stock values fell drastically, and many people went bankrupt because of their losses in the stock market. This chapter in U.S. history—and similar, less drastic economic and financial slumps—point out a type of risk known simply as "financial risk." Display **Visual 12.1**, which defines financial risk as the risk of losing principal—the amount invested or saved—and any earnings that have accrued to the principal.

12. Have the students go back to **Exercise 12.1** and decide what the financial risk is for each of these savings instruments. *(There is very little risk of loss of principal if a bank fails because FDIC insurance protects against loss for holders of savings accounts, certificates of deposits, and money market deposit accounts. The United States government stands behind the repayment of U.S. Savings Bonds.)*

CLOSURE

Remind the students that each type of savings or investment instrument carries risk.

Review these types of risk by asking the following questions:

- Describe inflation risk. *(This is the risk that the value of investments will not increase at least as rapidly as the rate of inflation.)*

- What types of savings instruments that we have studied would carry inflation risk? *(The only savings instrument discussed in this lesson that does not carry inflation risk is the Series I U.S. Saving Bond. All other savings instruments referenced in this lesson carry inflation risk.)*

- Describe interest rate risk. *(This is the risk that interest rates may change while the saver is "locked in" to savings instruments for a period of time.)*

- What types of savings instruments that we have studied would carry higher interest rate risk? *(Certificates of Deposit; Series EE U.S. Savings Bond issued on or after May 1, 2005.)*

- Describe risk of financial loss. *(This is the risk of losing principal and any earnings that have accrued to principal.)*

ASSESSMENT

Distribute to each student a copy of **Part 2: Weighting All the Risks** of **Assessment Lesson 12** from the *Student Workbook*. Have the students do the assessment, working independently.

Answers to Assessment Lesson 12:

1. Savings Accounts: Savings accounts carry an inflation risk. Even though the interest rate increases with the general increase in interest rates, the low rate on these accounts may not keep up with inflation.

2. Certificates of Deposit: The primary risks for a certificate of deposit (CD) are interest rate risk and inflation risk. These may be a problem if inflation and interest rates increase during the time the CD is held. On the other hand, a CD can be beneficial if inflation and interest rates decline during the time interval, because the rate is locked in.

3. U.S. Savings Bonds: Series EE bonds issued on or after May 1, 2005, experience inflation and interest rate risk since their rate of return is locked in. Series I bond rates will keep pace with inflation, but rates may decrease during a period of declining general interest rates.

EXTENSION

Explain that this lesson illustrates how inflation poses a risk to savers. Savers might save their money for a certain item only to find that the price of the item has increased at a faster rate than their savings have grown.

Help the students better understand the effects of inflation by instructing them to ask their parents, grandparents, or older neighbors to recall the price of an item they used to buy and the approximate year in which they bought it. For example, grandparents might remember buying gasoline for 25 cents per gallon in 1971 or a candy bar for 15 cents in 1965.

When students have gathered prices, use the inflation calculator (see the section titled "What is a dollar worth?") at the Federal Reserve Bank of Minneapolis website http://www.minneapolis-fed.org/. Instruct students to enter the price of the item and year to see what the price would be today. Discuss any differences in the calculated price and the real current price by explaining that not all prices increase at the same rate. Some items increase greatly in price, some items increase slightly, and some prices even decrease. Inflation is measured by the Consumer Price Index, which reports changes in the average price level. The inflation calculator reflects the increase in the average price level over time.

Nothing Is Risk-Free

Inflation risk: Risk that the value of investments will not increase at least as rapidly as the rate of inflation.

Interest rate risk: Risk that interest rates may change while the saver is "locked in" to a time deposit.

Financial risk: Risk of losing principal (the amount of money invested), and the return on the principal.

Who Pays and Who Receives?

LESSON DESCRIPTION AND BACKGROUND

The students discover that three factors affect how money grows in savings accounts: the amount deposited, the interest rate, and the length of time the money is held on deposit. Students calculate interest and formulate a generalization about the difference between simple and compound interest.

Lesson 13 is correlated with national standards for mathematics and economics, and with personal finance guidelines, as shown in Tables 1-3 in the introductory section of this publication.

ECONOMIC AND PERSONAL FINANCE CONCEPTS

- Compounding
- Compound interest
- Interest
- Interest rate
- Opportunity cost
- Rule of 72
- Simple interest

OBJECTIVES

At the end of this lesson, the student will be able to:

- Calculate **simple** and **compound interest**.
- Explain the **opportunity cost** of allowing interest to compound.
- Explain the **opportunity cost** of taking **interest** as it is earned.
- Analyze the difference between **simple** and **compound interest**.
- Explain the factors that affect how money grows.
- Apply the **Rule of 72**.

TIME REQUIRED

Two 45-minute class periods

MATERIALS

- A transparency of **Visual 13.1**, **13.2A**, **13.2B**, **13.3A**, **13.3B**, **13.4**, **13.5** and **13.6**

- A copy for each student of **Introduction** and **Vocabulary** sections of **Lesson 13** from the *Student Workbook*

- Copies of **Exercise 13.1A** (enough for half the class) and **13.1B** (enough for half the class)

- One copy for each student of **Exercise 13.2**, **13.3**, and **13.4** from the *Student Workbook*

- One copy for each student of **Lesson 13 Assessment** from the *Student Workbook*

- A bag of large dried kidney beans (or other beans of fairly uniform size)

- Two tall, narrow clear glasses or jars (one labeled "Simple Interest," the other labeled "Compound Interest")

- One small, narrow clear glass or jar (labeled "Interest Paid Out to Depositor")

- Two overhead projectors

- Calculators (one for each student)

ADDITIONAL RESOURCES

To download visuals, find related lessons, correlations to state standards, interactives, and more, visit http://fffl.councilforeconed.org/6-8/lesson13.

PROCEDURE

1. Introduce the concept of "interest" by asking if any students have a savings account. If any students do, ask why they keep their money in a savings account instead of a dresser drawer or a shoebox in their closets. *(Some students will know that banks provide security and pay interest on savings. Discuss these concepts to make sure students understand them.)*

2. Distribute a copy of the **Introduction** and **Vocabulary** section to **Lesson 13** from the *Student Workbook* to each student. Ask the students to read the passage and study the vocabulary words. When they are done with this, display **Visual 13.1**. Discuss the definitions it presents. Make sure the students understand the difference between simple and compound interest.

3. Explain that some people who earn interest on their savings leave that interest in the bank, in their savings accounts. When they do that, the interest usually "compounds", and savings grow.

4. Explain that some people need the interest they earn to pay for goods and services. They may not want to leave all of it in the bank to compound. If they withdraw their interest—if they "take it as it is earned"—their savings will grow more slowly.

5. Introduce the following simulation activity, designed to show the difference between simple and compound interest.

a. Divide the class into two groups: Simple Interest Group and Compound Interest Group. Give each student in the Simple Interest Group a copy of **Exercise 13.1A** from the *Student Workbook*; give each student in the Compound Interest Group a copy of **Exercise 13.1B**.

b. Give one narrow, tall glass or jar labeled "Simple Interest" and the smaller glass or jar labeled "Interest Paid Out to Depositor" to the Simple Interest Group. Give the other narrow, tall glass or jar, labeled "Compound Interest", to the Compound Interest Group.

c. Display **Visuals 13.2A** and **13.2B** side-by-side on the two overhead projectors.

d. Choose two students, one from each group, to act as bankers. Give each banker a bag of beans. Have each banker count 10 beans from the "bank bag" into his or her group's jar (labeled Simple Interest or Compound Interest). Have the rest of the students note the deposit in Column C on their charts on **Exercise 13.1A** or **13.1B**; point this out on the visuals.

e. Tell the students that the interest rate is 20 percent. Explain that this is an unusually high rate of interest, but it makes the calculations easier to perform and it will not affect the concept to be learned.

f. Instruct the bankers to take two beans from their respective bags to represent the 20 percent interest rate. The Simple Interest banker should put the two beans in the jar marked "Interest Paid Out to Depositor." The Compound Interest banker should put two beans into the jar marked "Compound Interest." (20 percent of 10 = .2 x 10 = 2; make sure the students understand that they must convert interest into decimal form when calculating interest earned.)

g. Explain that when interest is allowed to compound, it is added to the existing balance; as part of the new balance, it also earns interest. When interest is paid out to the depositor, it does not compound.

h. Have both groups look at their ending balance (Column G). Because the Compound Interest Group kept its interest on deposit, it has 12 beans; the Simple Interest Group has only 10.

i. Continue to work through the deposit cycle. (Deposit 10 beans, calculate interest, add "interest beans" to correct jar.) Have each group calculate its new balance (Column D), interest earned (Column F) and ending balance (Column G). Have the students complete six cycles. You can complete the visuals as the students calculate each cycle. Note: Decimals should be rounded to their nearest whole number.

j. Have the students count the beans in the compound interest jar (there should be 119) and in the two jars for the Simple Interest group. (They should have 60 beans in the deposit jar and 42 beans in the Interest Paid Out jar, for a total of 102.) Double check their answers by having the students calculate the total amount deposited in column C, and the total interest earned in column F.

6. Display **Visuals 13.3A** and **B**, Answer Sheets (or use the transparency you have with the written answers). Note that the Simple Interest Group and the Compound Interest Group each deposited the same amount, 60 beans. However, the Compound Interest Group earned a total of 59 beans in interest, but the Simple Interest Group earned only 42 beans. Ask:

a. What was the "opportunity cost" for the Simple Interest Group as it chose to receive its interest rather than leaving it on deposit, in the account? *(The opportunity cost was the extra interest they would have earned.)*

b. What was the opportunity cost for the Compound Interest Group as it chose to leave its interest on deposit, in the account? *(The opportunity cost was not being able to spend the interest at the present time. Remind the students, in connection with this point, that savers sometimes choose not to let interest compound because they have important uses in the present for*

that interest.)

7. Point out that the compound interest group not only received interest on the money they saved; they also earned interest on the interest the bank paid them. Display **Visual 13.4**. Ask:

a. How much money was deposited in Deposit Cycle 1? *($10)*

b. How much money was deposited in the remaining deposit cycles? *(0)*

c. What is the current Ending Balance? *($29.87)*

d. How much of the Ending Balance was deposited by the saver? *($10)*

e. How much of the Ending Balance is the result of interest earned? *($19.87)*

8. Look back at the previous example from **Visual 13.4**. Tell the students to assume that the saver earned the $10 referred to in Deposit Cycle 1 by working, and then deposited it in the bank. Ask: What job might you perform to earn $10? *(Some students might be able to earn $10 by cutting someone's lawn, shoveling snow, babysitting, etc.)* Point out that the saver in **Visual 13.4** has an Ending Balance of $29.87 in the account, but only had to work for $10 of that amount. The rest was paid in interest by the bank. The saver earned interest on the interest that the bank had paid in the earlier cycles.

Answers to Exercise 13.2

Principal	x	Interest Rate	x	Time	=	Simple Interest	÷ 4 =	Quarterly Payments
$60,000	x	6%	x	1 Year	=	$3,600	÷ 4 =	$900
$20,000	x	5%	x	1 Year	=	**$1,000**	÷ 4 =	**$250**
$10,000	x	10%	x	1 Year	=	$1,000	÷ 4 =	**$250**
$80,000	x	**7%**	x	1 Year	=	$5,600	÷ 4 =	**$1,400**
$75,000	x	9%	x	1 Year	=	**$6,750**	÷ 4 =	**$1,688**
$125,000	x	8%	x	1 Year	=	**$10,000**	÷ 4 =	**$2,500**
$200,000	x	**7%**	x	1 Year	=	$14,000	÷ 4 =	**$3,500**
$40,000	x	**5%**	x	1 Year	=	**$2,000**	÷ 4 =	$500
$100,000	x	4%	x	1 Year	=	**$4,000**	÷ 4 =	$1,000
$100,000	x	**10%**	x	1 Year	=	**$10,000**	÷ 4 =	$2,500

9. Explain that as savings grow while interest accrues, three important factors affect the amount of interest gained. Display **Visual 13.5** and discuss its contents. Make sure the students understand how the amount of money left on deposit, length of time money is left on deposit, and "interest rate" affect the interest earned.

10. Distribute to each student a copy of **Exercise 13.2** from the *Student Workbook*. Have the students complete the exercise, working independently. (Answers at the bottom of the previous page.)

11. Introduce **Exercise 13.3,** designed to show how the three factors—time, interest rate, and amount saved—affect the way money grows.

a. Distribute to each student a copy of **Exercise 13.3** from the *Student Workbook*. Go over the directions. Assign each student in each team one of the eight situations. (Or make up teams of eight students and have each student on each team select a different situation.) Have each student complete the Calculation Sheet for Racing Toward a Goal to determine when his or her driver will meet the goal. Students could use calculators or a spreadsheet program to do the calculations.

b. When the students have completed their calculations, they should compare their findings with their classmates' (or team's) findings to determine the correct order in which the drivers reached their goals. (Answers follow.)

The correct order of racers is:

F H E G B C D A

(Completed calculation sheets for each racer are found below and on the following pages.)

Answer grid for $2,000 at 6% interest. Racer A reaches the goal of $40,000 in 13 years.

A	B	C	D	E	F	G
Year	Beginning Balance (from G)	Annual Deposit	New Balance (B + C)	Interest Rate	Interest Earned (D x E)	Total (D + F)
1	0	$2,000	$2,000.00	6%	$120.00	$2,120.00
2	$2,120.00	$2,000	$4,120.00	6%	$247.20	$4,367.20
3	$4,367.20	$2,000	$6,367.20	6%	$382.03	$6,749.23
4	$6,749,23	$2,000	$8,749.23	6%	$524.95	$9,274.19
5	$9,274.19	$2,000	$11,274.19	6%	$676.45	$11,950.64
6	$11,950.64	$2,000	$13,950.64	6%	$837.04	$14,787.68
7	$14,787.68	$2,000	$16,787.68	6%	$1,007.26	$17,794.94
8	$17,794.94	$2,000	$19,794.94	6%	$1,187.70	$20,982.64
9	$20,982.64	$2,000	$22,982.64	6%	$1,378.96	$24,361.60
10	$24,361.60	$2,000	$26,361.60	6%	$1,581.70	$27,943.30
11	$27,943.30	$2,000	$29,943.30	6%	$1,796.60	$31,739.90
12	$31,739.90	$2,000	$33,739.90	6%	$2,024.39	$35,764.29
13	$35,764.29	$2,000	$37,764.29	6%	$2,265.86	$40,030.15

Answer grid for $2,000 at 10% interest. Racer B reaches the goal of $29,000 in 9 years.

A	B	C	D	E	F	G
Year	Beginning Balance (from G)	Annual Deposit	New Balance (B + C)	Interest Rate	Interest Earned (D x E)	Total (D + F)
1	0	$2,000	$2,000.00	10%	$200.00	$2,200.00
2	$2,200.00	$2,000	$4,200.00	10%	$420.00	$4,620.00
3	$4,620.00	$2,000	$6,620.00	10%	$662.00	$7,282.00
4	$7,282.00	$2,000	$9,282.00	10%	$928.20	$10,210.20
5	$10,210.20	$2,000	$12,210.20	10%	$1,221.02	$13,431.22
6	$13,431.22	$2,000	$15,431.22	10%	$1,543.12	$16,974.34
7	$16,974.34	$2,000	$18,974.34	10%	$1,897.43	$20,871.77
8	$20,871.77	$2,000	$22,871.77	10%	$2,287.18	$25,158.95
9	$25,158.95	$2,000	$27,158.95	10%	$2,715.90	$29,874.85

Answer grid for $3,000 at 6% interest. Racer C reaches the goal of $41,000 in 10 years.

A	B	C	D	E	F	G
Year	Beginning Balance (from G)	Annual Deposit	New Balance (B + C)	Interest Rate	Interest Earned (D x E)	Total (D + F)
1	0	$3,000	$3,000.00	6%	$180.00	$3,180.00
2	$3,180.00	$3,000	$6,180.00	6%	$370.80	$6,550.80
3	$6,550.80	$3,000	$9,550.80	6%	$573.05	$10,123.85
4	$10,123.85	$3,000	$13,123.85	6%	$787.43	$13,911.28
5	$13,911.28	$3,000	$16,911.28	6%	$1,014.68	$17,925.96
6	$17,925.96	$3,000	$20,925.96	6%	$1,255.56	$22,181.52
7	$22,181.52	$3,000	$25,181.52	6%	$1,510.89	$26,692.41
8	$26,692.41	$3,000	$29,692.41	6%	$1,781.54	$31,473.95
9	$31,473.95	$3,000	$34,473.95	6%	$2,068.44	$36,542.39
10	$36,542.39	$3,000	$39,542.39	6%	$2,372.54	$41,914.93

Answer grid for $3,000 at 10% interest. **Racer D** reaches the goal of $61,000 in 11 years.

A	B	C	D	E	F	G
Year	Beginning Balance (from G)	Annual Deposit	New Balance (B + C)	Interest Rate	Interest Earned (D x E)	Total (D + F)
1	0	$3,000	$3,000.00	10%	$300.00	$3,300.00
2	$3,300.00	$3,000	$6,300.00	10%	$630.00	$6,930.00
3	$6,930.00	$3,000	$9,930.00	10%	$993.00	$10,923.00
4	$10,923.00	$3,000	$13,923.00	10%	$1,392.30	$15,315.30
5	$15,315.30	$3,000	$18,513.30	10%	$1,831.53	$20,146.83
6	$20,146.83	$3,000	$23,146.83	10%	$2,314.68	$25,461.51
7	$25,461.51	$3,000	$28,461.51	10%	$2,846.15	$31,307.66
8	$31,307.66	$3,000	$34,307.66	10%	$3,430.77	$37,738.43
9	$37,738.43	$3,000	$40,738.43	10%	$4,073.84	$44,812.27
10	$44,812.27	$3,000	$47,812.27	10%	$4,781.23	$52,593.50
11	$52,593.50	$3,000	$55,593.50	10%	$5,559.35	$61,152.85

Answer grid for $4,000 at 6% interest. **Racer E** reaches the goal of $35,000 in 7 years.

A	B	C	D	E	F	G
Year	Beginning Balance (from G)	Annual Deposit	New Balance (B + C)	Interest Rate	Interest Earned (D x E)	Total (D + F)
1	0	$4,000	$4,000.00	6%	$240.00	$4,240.00
2	$4,240.00	$4,000	$8,240.00	6%	$494.40	$8,734.40
3	$8,734.40	$4,000	$12,734.40	6%	$764.06	$13,498.46
4	$13,498.46	$4,000	$17,498.46	6%	$1,049.91	$18,548.37
5	$18,548.37	$4,000	$22,548.37	6%	$1,352.90	$23,901.27
6	$23,901.27	$4,000	$27,901.27	6%	$1,674.08	$29,575.35
7	$29,575.35	$4,000	$33,575.35	6%	$2,014.52	$35,589.87

Answer grid for $4,000 at 10% interest. **Racer F** reaches the goal of $26,000 in 5 years.

A	B	C	D	E	F	G
Year	Beginning Balance (from G)	Annual Deposit	New Balance (B + C)	Interest Rate	Interest Earned (D x E)	Total (D + F)
1	0	$4,000	$4,000.00	10%	$400.00	$4,400.00
2	$4,400.00	$4,000	$8,400.00	10%	$840.00	$9,240.00
3	$9,240.00	$4,000	$13,240.00	10%	$1,324.00	$14,564.00
4	$14,564.00	$4,000	$18,564.00	10%	$1,856.40	$20,420.40
5	$20,420.40	$4,000	$24,420.40	10%	$2,442.04	$26,862.44

Answer grid for $5,000 at 6% interest. **Racer G** reaches the goal of $52,000 in 8 years.

A	B	C	D	E	F	G
Year	Beginning Balance (from G)	Annual Deposit	New Balance (B + C)	Interest Rate	Interest Earned (D x E)	Total (D + F)
1	0	$5,000	$5,000.00	6%	$300.00	$5,300.00
2	$5,300.00	$5,000	$10,300.00	6%	$618.00	$10,918.00
3	$10,918.00	$5,000	$15,918.00	6%	$955.08	$16,373.08
4	$16,873.08	$5,000	$21,873.08	6%	$1,312.38	$23,185.46
5	$23,185.46	$5,000	$28,185.46	6%	$1,691.13	$29,876.59
6	$29,876.59	$5,000	$34,876.59	6%	$2,092.60	$36,969.19
7	$36,969.19	$5,000	$41,969.19	6%	$2,518.15	$44,487.34
8	$44,487.34	$5,000	$49,487.34	6%	$2,969.24	$52,456.58

Answer grid for $5,000 at 10% interest. **Racer H** reaches the goal of $42,000 in 6 years.

A	B	C	D	E	F	G
Year	Beginning Balance (from G)	Annual Deposit	New Balance (B + C)	Interest Rate	Interest Earned (D x E)	Total (D + F)
1	0	$5,000	$5,000.00	10%	$500.00	$5,500.00
2	$5,500.00	$5,000	$10,500.00	10%	$1,050.00	$11,550.00
3	$11,550.00	$5,000	$16,550.00	10%	$1,655.00	$18,205.00
4	$18,205.00	$5,000	$23,205.00	10%	$2,320.50	$25,525.50
5	$25,525.50	$5,000	$30,525.50	10%	$3,052.55	$33,578.05
6	$33,578.05	$5,000	$38,578.05	10%	$3,857.81	$42,435.86

FINANCIAL FITNESS FOR LIFE: Teacher Guide Grades 6-8
http://fffl.councilforeconed.org/6-8

12. Explain that there is an easy way to estimate the extent to which interest compounds when it is left to accumulate. It is called the "Rule of 72." Using the Rule of 72 enables you to estimate how long it takes for money to double, at a given rate of interest. To use the rule, you divide the number 72 by the interest rate (expressed in percentage terms), and the answer is the approximate number of years required to double your money. For example, at 9 percent interest, money doubles in about 8 years (72 ÷ 9 = 8); at 2 percent interest, money doubles in about 36 years (72 ÷ 2 = 36).

13. How well does the Rule of 72 work? Distribute to each student a copy of **Exercise 13.4** from the *Student Workbook*. Have the students complete the exercise to find out how accurately the Rule of 72 predicts the time it will take for $100,000 to double at different interest rates.

- The students can use an online interest calculator such as the one found at www.1728.com/compint.htm to check out the Rule of 72.

- They should use this procedure:

  1. Solve for YEARS

  Input principal:100000 (do not use commas)

  Input total: 200000 (i.e., double the principal)

  Input rate (do not use a decimal, e.g. 6% = 6)

2. Click on CALCULATE

The answer will be the number of years it takes for the principal to double.

- Ask: Does the Rule of 72 Work? *(Students should observe that the Rule of 72 is fairly accurate in estimating the length of time needed for money to double. In each of the examples, money doubles approximately as predicted by the Rule of 72.)*

CLOSURE

Use the following questions to review the lesson:

- What is simple interest? *(Interest earned on the principal and paid out to the depositor.)*

- What is compound interest? *(Interest computed on the sum of the principle and previously earned interest.)*

- What determines the amount of interest earned? *(The interest rate, the amount deposited, and the length of time on which the interest is calculated.)*

- If you left $3,000 in a savings account earning 8% interest, approximately how many years would it take to double in size? *(Nine years, when estimated by the Rule of 72, or 72 ÷ 8 = 9.)*

Answers to Exercise 13.4

A	B	C	D	E
Principal	Double the Principal	Interest Rate Percentage	No. of years for money to double (from Web Calculator)	Does Column C x Column D = approximately 72?
$100,000	$200,000	2	35.0028	70.01
$100,000	$200,000	3	23.4498	70.35
$100,000	$200,000	4	17.673	70.69
$100,000	$200,000	6	11.8957	71.37
$100,000	$200,000	8	9.0065	72.05
$100,000	$200,000	9	8.0432	72.39
$100,000	$200,000	12	6.1163	73.4

ASSESSMENT

Distribute a copy of **Lesson 13 Assessment** to each student. Have the students complete the assessment, working independently. Answers are shown in **Visual 13.6**. You may want to request that the students round cents to the nearest whole number in performing their calculations.

EXTENSION

Introduce students to Future Value (a method for calculating the value of cash today at a specific date in the future) by using the equation $FV=PV(1+i)^n$.

Explain the variables as follows:

FV = Future Value (the value of the student's savings at some future date)

PV = Present Value (the current value of their savings)

i = the interest rate, expressed in decimal form, that the saver expects to receive for his savings

n = the number of years the saver will be earning interest by saving the money

Pose the following problem:

For high school graduation, Sarah received $2,000 in cash gifts, which she immediately placed in a 5-year Certificate of Deposit (CD) paying 4 percent (.04) annual interest. Approximately how much money will Sarah have when the CD matures in 5 years?

FV = ?

PV = $2,000

i = .04

n = 5

Put it all together as follows:

$FV = \$2,000(1 + .04)^5$

$FV = \$2,000(1.04)^5$

FV = $2,433.31

Provide similar scenarios using different interest rates and time periods to allow students to practice with the formula. Point out that small changes in interest rates and time periods can make big differences in the outcome.

Interesting Information about Interest

Interest

The price paid for using someone else's money.

Interest Rate

The price paid for using someone else's money expressed as a percentage.

Principal

Basic amount deposited, without adding interest earned.

Simple Interest

Interest earned on the principal and paid out to a depositor.

Compound Interest

Interest computed on the sum of the principal and previously earned interest.

Compounding

The practice of leaving interest earned on deposit, so that it also earns interest.

Simple Interest

A	B	C	D	E	F	G
Deposit Cycle	Beginning Balance (from previous G)	Deposited Amount	New Balance (B + C)	Rate of Interest	Interest Earned and paid out (D x E)	Ending Balance (D)
1	0	10	10	20%	2	10
2		10		20%		
3		10		20%		
4		10		20%		
5		10		20%		
6		10		20%		
Total						

FINANCIAL FITNESS FOR LIFE: Teacher Guide Grades 6-8
http://fffl.councilforeconed.org/6-8

Compound Interest

A	B	C	D	E	F	G
Deposit Cycle	Beginning Balance (from previous G)	Deposited Amount	New Balance (B + C)	Rate of Interest	Interest Earned and paid out (D x E)	Ending Balance (F + D)
1	0	10	10	20%	2	12
2		10		20%		
3		10		20%		
4		10		20%		
5		10		20%		
6		10		20%		
Total						

Round decimals to the closest whole number.

Answers to Exercise 13.1A
Simple Interest

A Deposit Cycle	B Beginning Balance (from previous G)	C Deposited Amount	D New Balance (B + C)	E Rate of Interest	F Interest Earned and paid out (D x E)	G Ending Balance (D)
1	0	10	10	20%	2	10
2	10	10	20	20%	4	20
3	20	10	30	20%	6	30
4	30	10	40	20%	8	40
5	40	10	50	20%	10	50
6	50	10	60	20%	12	60
Total		60			42	

FINANCIAL FITNESS FOR LIFE: Teacher Guide Grades 6-8
http://fffl.councilforeconed.org/6-8

Answers to Exercise 13.1B
Compound Interest

A	B	C	D	E	F	G
Deposit Cycle	Beginning Balance (from previous G)	Deposited Amount	New Balance (B + C)	Rate of Interest	Interest Earned and paid out (D x E)	Ending Balance (F + D)
1	0	10	10	20%	2	12
2	**12**	10	**22**	20%	**4**	**26**
3	**26**	10	**36**	20%	**7**	**43**
4	**43**	10	**53**	20%	**11**	**64**
5	**64**	10	**74**	20%	**15**	**89**
6	**89**	10	**99**	20%	**20**	**119**
Total		60			59	

Round decimals to the closest whole number.

The Bank's Contribution

A	B	C	D	E	F	G
Deposit Cycle	Beginning Balance (from previous G)	Deposited Amount	New Balance (B + C) Rate of Interest	Rate of Interest	Interest Earned and left in account (D x E)	Ending Balance (F + D)
1	0	10	10.00	20%	2.00	12.00
2	12.00	0	12.00	20%	2.40	14.40
3	14.40	0	14.40	20%	2.88	17.28
4	17.28	0	17.28	20%	3.46	20.74
5	20.74	0	20.74	20%	4.15	24.89
6	24.89	0	24.89	20%	4.98	29.87
Total		10			19.87	29.87

Factors That Affect How Money Grows

- Amount of money left on deposit

- Interest rate

- Length of time money is left on deposit

Lesson 13 Assessment:
Answer Key

Beginning values:
Amount $5,000
Interest rate 5%
Time 5 years

Change only the amount:
Amount $10,000
Interest rate 5%
Time 5 years

Change only the interest rate:
Amount $5,000
Interest rate 10%
Time 5 years

Change only the time:
Amount $5,000
Interest rate 5%
Time 10 years

Year	Year Start Balance	Interest Rate	Interest Earned	Year End Balance
1	$5,000	5%	$250.00	$5,250.00
2	5,250.00	5%	262.50	5,512.50
3	5,512.50	5%	275.63	5,788.13
4	5,788.13	5%	289.41	6,077.54
5	6,077.54	5%	303.88	6,381.42
1	$10,000.0	5%	500.00	10,500.00
2	10,500.00	5%	525.00	11,025.00
3	11,025.00	5%	551.25	11,576.25
4	11,576.25	5%	578.81	12,155.06
5	12,155.06	5%	607.75	12,762.81
1	$5,000.00	10%	500.00	5,500.00
2	5,500.00	10%	550.00	6,050.00
3	6,050.00	10%	605.00	6,655.00
4	6,655.00	10%	665.50	7,320.50
5	7,320.50	10%	732.05	8,052.55
1	$5,000.00	5%	250.00	5,250.00
2	5,250.00	5%	262.50	5,512.50
3	5,512.50	5%	275.63	5,788.13
4	5,788.13	5%	289.41	6,077.54
5	6,077.54	5%	303.88	6,381.42
6	6,381.42	5%	319.07	6,700.49
7	6,700.49	5%	335.02	7,035.51
8	7,035.51	5%	351.78	7,389.29
9	7,387.29	5%	369.36	7,756.65
10	7,756.65	5%	387.83	8,144.48

If rounding of cents to the nearest whole number is not completed in each year, the answers will vary from the answer key.

Stocks and Mutual Funds

LESSON DESCRIPTION AND BACKGROUND

The students learn about stocks—how stocks are issued, different levels of risk, and differences in possible returns. In studying risk, the students also learn about mutual funds and diversification.

Lesson 14 is correlated with national standards for mathematics and economics, and with personal finance guidelines, as shown in Tables 1-3 in the introductory section of this publication.

ECONOMIC AND PERSONAL FINANCE CONCEPTS

- Capital gains
- Diversification
- Dividend
- Equity
- Mutual funds
- Risk
- Stocks

OBJECTIVES

At the end of this lesson, the student will be able to:

- Explain that **stocks** represent shares of ownership in a corporation.
- Explain the **risk** associated with stock ownership.
- Explain two ways in which stocks provide a return to owners: **capital gains** and **dividends**.
- Define **mutual funds**; identify different types of mutual funds.
- Define **diversification**.

TIME REQUIRED

Two 45-minute class periods

MATERIALS

- A transparency of **Visual 14.1** and **14.2**
- A copy for each student of **Introduction** and **Vocabulary** sections of **Lesson 14** from the *Student Workbook*
- A copy for each student of **Exercise 14.1** from the *Student Workbook*. Distribute copies to the five cast members a day ahead of time (see **Procedure 2**)
- A copy for each student of **Exercise 14.2**, **14.3**, and **14.4** from the *Student Workbook*
- Two small boxes (see **Procedure 20**)
- The financial pages of a newspaper
- Six sheets of poster board
- Art supplies
- Magazines

ADDITIONAL RESOURCES

To download visuals, find related lessons, correlations to state standards, interactives, and more, visit http://fffl.councilforeconed.org/6-8/lesson14

PROCEDURE

1. Distribute a copy of the **Introduction** and **Vocabulary** sections of **Lesson 14** from the *Student Workbook* to each student. Introduce the lesson's focus on stocks and mutual funds and ask the students to read the handout. Explain briefly that some investors put their money into buying stocks. When they buy stocks from a given company, they become part-owners of that company. If the company does well, they will benefit. But if the company does not do well, they may lose some or all of the money they invested. To guard against this risk of loss,

many investors diversify. That means they spread their investments around, buying stock in several companies. In order to diversify, many investors invest in mutual funds.

2. Explain that the lesson will begin with a play that illustrates some main points about investing in stocks. You have arranged for five students to perform a play about two pie companies in competition with one another. Distribute copies of **Exercise 14.1** (the cast members will have received their copies in advance). Invite the other class members to read along with the performance. When the play has been performed, the students should answer the two questions that follow the exercise. Discuss the answers as follows:

a. Why did Perfect Pies become more profitable than Pretty Pies? *(Perfect Pies bought a crust-making machine and a fruit-slicing machine. These are investments in capital which increase productivity and improve the company's potential to be profitable.)*

b. What will Pretty Pies have to do to compete with Perfect Pies? *(Pretty Pies will have to invest in capital also.)*

3. Display **Visual 14.1**. Explain that this chart represents an apple pie from Perfect Pies. The pie is divided into 10 slices. It could be divided in other ways, such as two slices or four slices. Why do people divide pies into slices? *(So that many people can have some.)*

4. Explain that when we slice the pie and give some to others, we are sharing. We are giving people a share of the pie.

5. Explain that this pie chart represents the "value" of Perfect Pies. The company is valued at $10,000, so the pie chart represents $10,000. The owner of the company has decided to slice the company into 10 "shares." She offered one of those shares to Lydia. Ask: How much is each share worth? *($1,000)* Write "$1,000" in each slice on the chart.

6. Explain that when other investors began examining Perfect Pies, many of them wanted to buy some shares, too. So the owner kept two shares for herself and sold the remaining seven shares.

(Remind the students that Lydia still owns a share.)

7. Explain that as more investors saw the success of Perfect Pies, they also wanted shares. The owner was not willing to sell her last two shares, so the new investors contacted Lydia and the other seven investors and asked to buy their shares. Most of the original investors agreed to sell their shares, but only if the new investors were willing to give them $2,000 for each share. The new investors were willing. Ask the students what these purchases will do to the value of the company. *(It will increase the value of the company.)*

8. Display **Visual 14.2**. Write "$2,000" in each slice. Explain that each of the shares is now worth $2,000. Ask:

a. How much is the whole company worth? *(10 shares x $2,000 = $20,000)*

b. Did the number of slices change? *(No.)*

9. Emphasize the point that the number of slices/shares did not increase. Rather, the entire pie increased. Lay **Visual 14.2** on top of **Visual 14.1** to illustrate the increase in the size of the pie (or draw the circles on the board). Ask:

a. What is each share worth? *($2,000)*

b. What is Lydia's share worth? *($2,000)*

c. If Lydia sells her stock now, how much will she receive? *($2,000)*

d. How much did Lydia pay for the stock? *($1,000)*

e. In the play, how much did Lydia receive from the pie store owner? *($1,000 in the second year)*

10. Explain that there are two ways in which stocks may provide a return to their owners. One way is "capital gains." A capital gain is a profit somebody makes when he or she sells a stock (or another asset) for more than he or she paid for it. The other way is through "dividends." A dividend is a portion of a company's profit paid to stockholders. When the pie store owner paid Meredith $1,000, she was paying Meredith a dividend.

11. Explain that shares in Perfect Pies were exchanged directly between the buyer of the stock and the seller. However, stocks are usually bought and sold in the "stock market." The stock market serves an important purpose in our financial system. It provides us with information about the companies whose stock we might want to purchase.

12. Explain that in *The Pie War*, Pretty Pies and Perfect Pies seemed to be identical pie companies, but then something happened to make them different. Remind the students that Pretty Pies and Perfect Pies both received $1,000 from investors, and both were profitable. Perfect Pies took part of its "profit" (rather than paying Lydia $500 in dividends) and bought capital that would make it more efficient in pie production. Pretty Pies used part of its profit to pay a big dividend. Ask:

a. Which company did better in the long run? *(Perfect Pies.)*

b. Which stock did Kendall buy? *(Pretty Pies.)*

c. Why did Kendall buy stock in Pretty Pies? *(Because it paid a large dividend to Meredith.)*

13. Explain that the Pretty Pies stock Kendall purchased is not going to gain in value to the extent that the stock in Perfect Pies will gain. However, Kendall didn't have the right information, so she couldn't make a good decision about which stock to buy.

14. Distribute copies of **Exercise 14.2**; have the students read the exercise and answer the questions posed at the end. When they have completed their work, discuss their answers.

a. Which company's stock did research analysts recommend? *(Perfect Pies.)*

b. What was it about the Perfect Pies operations that impressed the analysts? *(Capital investment and the potential for long-term growth.)*

c. What was the signal to other stock purchasers that Perfect Pies was a good investment? *(Answers will vary. The increase in the*

price of its stock may have been a favorable sign, suggesting an improved outlook on the future profitability of Perfect Pies.)

d. What was the signal to other stock purchasers that Pretty Pies was not a good investment? *(Answers will vary. The stock price did not increase, which may have been an unfavorable sign for Pretty Pies.)*

15. Explain that investors face "risk" when they buy stock. Even a company as smart as Perfect Pies can experience problems. Sometimes companies' managers make mistakes. At other times, companies are hurt by events in the marketplace that are beyond the control of their managers.

16. Distribute copies of **Exercise 14.3** from the *Student Workbook*. Have the students complete the exercise and answer the questions. Discuss students' answers.

Scenario 1

a. If the pie company goes back to making the crusts by hand, will the "supply" of pies increase or decrease? *(The supply of pies will decrease. One of the reasons for the success of Perfect Pies was the adoption of the pie crust machine. The machine allowed the company to increase the rate at which it produced pies. It increased the company's productivity.)*

b. Is this a problem that can be controlled by management? *(Yes.)*

Scenario 2

a. If the pie company cannot get apples without worms, will the supply of apple pies increase or decrease? *(The supply of apple pies will decrease.)*

b. Is this a problem that can be controlled by management? *(Management cannot control this event. However, it might be able to mitigate the damages by increasing the production of other pie flavors. Some consumers may be willing to substitute.)*

Scenario 3

a. If the Pronly diet becomes popular, what will happen to the "demand" for apple pies? **(The demand for apple pies will decrease.)**

b. Is this a problem that can be controlled by management? **(No. However, the company may be able to wait out this fad diet.)**

17. Point out that owning a stock in a particular company can be risky. As an example, although Perfect Pies seems to be successful, various events could derail its progress. A fad diet, worn-out machines, and wormy apples are just three examples.

18. Explain that, for investors, one solution to this problem is to buy stock in several different companies. This is called "diversification." Diversification is the tactic of owning several different assets for the purpose of reducing risk. A fad protein diet may reduce the demand for pie, but at the same time it might increase the demand for meat. So, an investor might reduce his or her risk by owning stock in both the pie company and a meat company.

19. Explain that it takes a great deal of work to diversify by buying many individual stocks. Before they buy, smart investors spend time researching the companies in which they might be interested. They are watchful for events that could have a negative effect on the supply of or demand for products sold by the companies in which they might be interested. The stakes may be high for investors. Mistakes may be costly.

20. Explain that not all investors have the time or the expertise needed to diversify their holdings by researching and investing in several individual stocks. Many of them follow a different approach. Introduce the following activity as a simplified representation of this alternative. Gather a small box, a newspaper, and a pair of scissors. Place the box on your desk. Open a newspaper to the stock report page. Name a stock and say something like, "Hmm, IBM. I think I'll buy 10,000 shares of this." Cut a small chunk out of the paper and place it in the box.

Do this four or five times. Each time, mention a blue chip stock such as Boeing Company, McDonald's, Wal-Mart, or Coca-Cola.

21. Explain that you are acting as a fund manager for a mutual fund. A "mutual fund" is a collection of shares of stock from many companies, along with other financial investments and cash. As a "fund manager," you and your advisors pick the stocks and the amount of shares of the stocks to be included in the fund.

22. Explain that your goal as fund manager is to increase the value of the fund. By purchasing many different stocks, you reduce the risk that your fund will lose money; even if some stocks in your fund go down in value, other stocks in your fund may go up.

23. Investors can buy shares in mutual funds. In doing so, they become part-owners of all of the stocks held in the fund. Buying shares in a mutual fund provides instant diversification.

24. Place another small box on your desk. Go through the same procedure as described above—creating another mutual fund—but this time name stocks from smaller companies, such as Nuance Communication, Ladish, Mattson Technology, Arena Pharmaceuticals, or Mueller Industries. Ask the students if they have detected any difference between this fund and the other one. **(The students most likely will not have heard of the companies in the second fund.)**

25. Explain that the first fund contained all "blue chip stocks." These are stocks in big companies that have been doing a profitable business for a long time. A blue-chip mutual fund is likely, many investors believe, to provide sustained but relatively slow growth. It is regarded as a suitable investment for people who want to receive a regular income from their financial investments, don't want to risk losing large amounts of money, and are satisfied with relatively small, sustained gains in value.

26. Explain that the second fund invested in smaller companies that seem likely to prosper, though how well they actually will do in the future is uncertain. This sort of fund is called a

"growth fund", and it is riskier. It is most suitable for investors who are willing to risk losing some money, while hoping that these small companies will grow and that the stock will increase greatly in value.

27. Explain that there are many different kinds of mutual funds, and that different funds carry different levels of risk. There are overseas growth funds that invest in stocks in foreign companies. There are "green funds" that invest in stocks in businesses whose operations are environmentally friendly. Each mutual fund is designed to meet the investment goals of a particular type of investor.

28. To look further into mutual funds, distribute copies of **Exercise 14.4** from the *Student Workbook* to each student. Separate the students into small groups and have the groups complete the exercise by offering profiles of investors in income funds and growth funds. Discuss the profiles. *(Discussion points: People who would be wise to choose income funds, and the associated lower level of risk, are those who are nearing retirement or who are already retired and have no way to earn back any losses; people with lower wage levels; and people who have large financial commitments, such as near-term or current college tuition payments. People who could reasonably accept more risk include those who are young and therefore able to make up losses over time; people who earn high salaries; and people who have long time horizons for large financial obligations [such as a college fund for a two-year-old child].)*

CLOSURE

1. Remind the students that stocks offer an investor ownership in a company. As an owner, an investor faces the risk of losing part or all of the investment if the business fails. For that reason, an investor should purchase stocks carefully. If he or she is comfortable with a relatively high level of risk, the investor may want to purchase stock in a small or new company that shows great potential for growth. However, if an investor would rather have slow and steady growth, with less risk of losing his or her initial investment, stocks in stable, large companies would be preferred.

2. Ask the students what the following statement means: "Don't put all your eggs in one basket." The students should recognize that if anybody puts all his eggs in one basket, and the basket falls to the ground, all the eggs will be worthless. The same is true for stocks. It is important for investors to reduce their risk by having a number of diverse stocks. (Explain that diversification can also be accomplished by including other financial instruments, such as bonds and savings accounts, in an investment portfolio.)

3. Ask the following questions.

- What are stocks? *(Stocks are shares of ownership in a business.)*

- Why are stocks called equities? *(The word equity means ownership, and stocks represent ownership in a corporation.)*

- What are the risks associated with stock ownership? *(There is no guarantee of a return on your investment. The price of the stock could go up or down or gain more slowly than other financial investments gain. The company could go bankrupt, and in that case the stockholder would probably lose his or her entire investment.)*

- What are the returns for stocks? *(Dividends and capital gains.)*

ASSESSMENT

Write a one-page paper explaining what stocks are, the risk associated with stock ownership and ways to reduce this risk. *(Students should define stocks as shares of ownership, explain that stocks can decline in value over fairly long periods of time, and discuss diversification and mutual funds as ways to reduce risk.)*

EXTENSION

1. Explain that education offers many different areas of study. Students may study math, history, language arts, science, and other subject areas. Ask the students to consider what their adult lives would be like if all they learned in school were math. Explain that there is diversity in the education they receive. Education provides an analogy for the importance of diversity in investments.

2. Place the students in six groups. Tell them that they are to present an analogy of a diversified stock portfolio in collage form or in a drawing. Be sure that the students understand what an analogy is *(a comparison between two things, based on a correspondence or partial similarity)*. Provide the students with poster boards, magazines, and art supplies. Assign two groups each of the following topics: education, diet, and exercise. An education poster or drawing could depict a person's limited opportunities or abilities if he or she has studied only one subject area. A diet poster or collage could contain pictures of many types of foods representing a diversified diet that helps people remain healthy. An exercise poster or collage could include a depiction of what a person would look like if he or she only performed leg exercises at the gym.

3. Have the members of each group make an oral presentation of their analogy, explaining why a diversified stock portfolio is important for financial health and well-being.

A Pie Chart

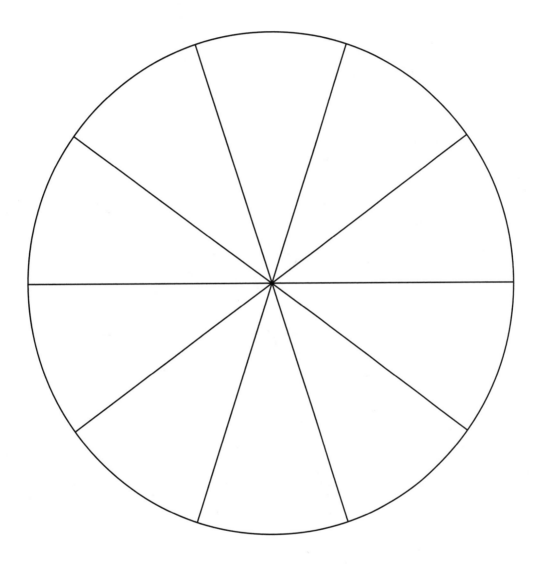

Building a Bigger Pie

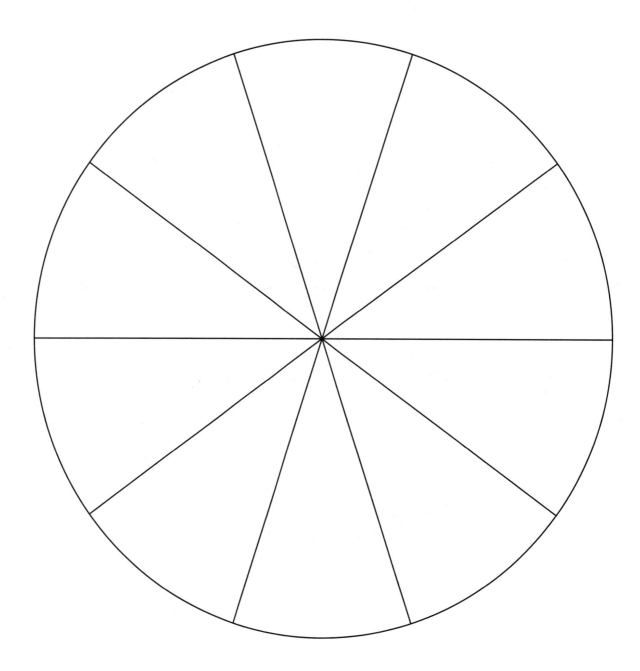

FINANCIAL FITNESS FOR LIFE: Teacher Guide Grades 6-8
http://fffl.councilforeconed.org/6-8

Cash or Credit?

LESSON DESCRIPTION AND BACKGROUND

Most students are aware of the variety of payment options available to consumers. Cash, checks, debit cards, and credit cards are often used by their parents; however, the students probably do not understand the implications of each. This lesson examines the advantages and disadvantages of various payment methods and focuses especially on using credit. The students are challenged to calculate the cost of credit, compare credit card agreements, and analyze case studies to determine whether credit is being used wisely.

Lesson 15 is correlated with national standards for mathematics and economics, and with personal finance guidelines, as shown in Tables 1-3 in the introductory section of this publication.

ECONOMIC AND PERSONAL FINANCE CONCEPTS

- Annual fee
- APR
- Credit limit
- Finance charge
- Grace period
- Inflation
- Interest
- Interest rate
- Late fee
- Minimum payment
- Opportunity cost

OBJECTIVES

At the end of this lesson, the student will be able to:

- Differentiate between forms of cash payment and credit.

- Compare the advantages and disadvantages of using credit.
- Explain how **interest** is calculated.
- Analyze the **opportunity cost** of using credit and various forms of cash payments.
- Evaluate the costs and benefits of various credit card agreements.

TIME REQUIRED

Two or three 45-minute class periods

MATERIALS

- A transparency of **Visual 15.1**, **15.2**, and **15.3**

- A copy for each student of **Introduction to Theme 5** and **Introduction** and **Vocabulary** sections of **Lesson 15** from the *Student Workbook*

- A copy for each student of **Exercise 15.1**, **15.2**, and **15.3** from the *Student Workbook*

- A copy for each student of **Lesson 15 Assessment** from the *Student Workbook*

- Credit card application forms—one for each student. Collect these ahead of time, or have students bring in those their parents receive.

- A calculator for each student

ADDITIONAL RESOURCES

To download visuals, find related lessons, correlations to state standards, interactives, and more, visit http://fffl.councilforeconed.org/6-8/lesson15.

PROCEDURE

1. Distribute a copy of **Introduction to Theme 5** and **Introduction** and **Vocabulary** sections of **Lesson 15** in the *Student Workbook* to each student. Have the students read the handouts

and introduce the lesson by asking the students to name some different ways people can pay for goods and services. Guide their responses to make sure that credit is one of them. *(Possible responses should include cash, check, debit card, gift certificate, credit card.)* Display **Visual 15.1** and write their suggestions in the left-hand column.

2. Ask the students to suggest advantages and disadvantages of each payment method. Write their ideas on **Visual 15.1**. *(Suggested answers are in the table below.)*

3. Explain that cash, checks, and debit cards are forms of "money." They can be used as a medium of exchange (a means of payment) in most transactions.

4. Explain that "credit" is not money, but is actually a loan. When a person uses a credit card, his or her signature on the credit receipt verifies an agreement to pay back the money at a later date, with "interest" if the loan is not paid by a certain time.

5. Display **Visual 15.2** and **Visual 15.3**. Discuss the processes, making sure the students understand that a "check" is drawn on an

Answers to Visual 15.1

Payment Options	Advantages	Disadvantages
Currency (Paper Money)	*Fast, no paperwork, acceptable in most situations*	*Can be stolen or lost; consumer might not have enough. Cannot be used for telephone or Internet purchases. Should not be used in paying bills by mail.*
Coins	*Fast, no paperwork, acceptable in most situations*	*Heavy, can be stolen or lost, only useful for small purchases. Cannot be used for telephone or Internet purchases. Should not be used in paying bills by mail.*
Gift Certificate	*Just like currency*	*Only good at a specific store; user may need identification. May have expiration date.*
Debit Card	*Safe, confidential, user not responsible for all purchases made on stolen card, no need to carry cash.*	*Must record each purchase amount; limited by amount in checking account. Need to remember PIN. May not be acceptable everywhere.*
Credit Card	*Safe, user not responsible for all purchases made on stolen card. Can be used for telephone and Internet purchases. Can be used in paying bills by mail.*	*User must pay interest for late payments; user may incur fees if balance not paid by due date. May not be accepted everywhere.*
Smart Card	*Can be used as credit or debit card. Same as debit card and credit card. May also be used as identification. Better security. Can store cash, too.*	*If used as debit card - same. If used as credit card - same.*

existing account; credit is an I.O.U.—a loan—that must be repaid, sometimes with interest.

6. Review the concept of "opportunity cost", the next-best alternative given up when a choice is made. Ask what Chad's opportunity cost was when he spent $50 at the music shop and paid with a check. **(He gave up the opportunity to earn interest on the $50 or to buy something else with the $50—whichever would have been his next choice.)**

7. Ask what Chad's opportunity cost was when he bought the video games and used his credit card. **(His opportunity cost lies in the future. He will have to give up the opportunity to buy something else with the $50 he must pay back when the credit card bill comes due.)**

8. Introduce an important personal finance decision: Choosing a credit card.

a. Display a number of credit card applications that you have clearly marked "VOID" and from which you have deleted personal information—or have students go to www.bankrate.com to get examples of different credit card offers. Review the relevant vocabulary **(annual fee, annual percentage rate, grace period, interest rate, minimum payment, etc.)**

b. Distribute one application to each student, along with a copy of **Exercise 15.1** from the *Student Workbook*. Have the students work in pairs, using their two applications to complete **Exercise 15.1**. **(Answers will vary. The students should note that they need to analyze all aspects of an offer—interest rate, grace period, minimum payment, etc.—before deciding which offer is best.)**

c. Explain that choosing a credit card should be like choosing any other good or service. People should shop around and compare different credit cards before making a decision.

d. Explain that credit offers consumers the opportunity to enjoy a product in the present and pay for it later. This can be especially ad-

vantageous when a consumer buys something at a sale price—one that will be raised to a higher price later.

e. The downside? For some cardholders, there is no downside. They watch their spending and pay their credit card bills on time, avoiding interest charges. For others, however, access to credit can lead to impulse buying and to buyers' remorse when the bill at the end of the month is too steep to be paid.

9. Explain that many factors come into play for consumers as they make their choices about paying in cash or buying on credit. The four cases described in **Exercise 15.2** from the *Student Workbook* illustrate many of these factors. Distribute a copy of the exercise to each student. Also distribute calculators and review the math processes required to calculate interest. Then have the students work in pairs to complete the exercise. (If your students are proficient with spreadsheets, you may wish to have them construct a spreadsheet to complete this activity.) Answers follow.

Answers to Exercise 15.2:

A. *Elizabeth: Because of inflation, the computer will cost $1,030 a year later. Elizabeth will save $1,080; she will be able to buy the computer and will have $50 (plus interest) left over.*

B. *David: Will pay back the $800 in one month; he will pay no interest.*

C. *Ryan: It will take Ryan 10 months to pay off his credit card debt; he will have spent $865.18 on the laptop, including interest. The calculations are shown on the following page.*

D. *Caitlin: Paying only the minimum monthly payment, it will take Caitlin almost 11 years (131÷12) to pay her credit card debt, and she will have paid $1,615.49 for the laptop, which includes interest of $815.49.*

10. Ask the students to compare the choices made by the four consumers and decide who made the best decision. (*David's choice appears to be best. David got the enjoyment of his computer right away; and because he paid his credit card balance in full, he paid no interest. Elizabeth had to wait a year to begin enjoying her computer; and her cost was $1,030. Ryan got to enjoy his new computer while he made his monthly payments, but his total cost was $865.18. Caitlin got to enjoy her new computer right away; but it took her about 11 years to pay for it, and* the total cost was more than $1,600. The students may comment that Caitlin will undoubtedly want a newer and better computer before she finishes paying for the one she just bought.)

Answers to Exercise 15.2, Ryan's Credit Card Summary

A	B	C	D	E	F
No. of Months	Amount Owed	$90 paid each month	Monthly Interest Paid (B x .015)	Principal Paid (C-D)	New Balance
Month 1	$800.00	$90.00	$12.00	$78.00	$722.00
Month 2	$722.00	$90.00	$10.83	$79.17	$642.83
Month 3	*$642.83*	*$90.00*	*$9.64*	*$80.36*	*$562.47*
Month 4	*$562.47*	*$90.00*	*$8.44*	*$81.56*	*$480.91*
Month 5	*$480.91*	*$90.00*	*$7.21*	*$82.79*	*$398.12*
Month 6	*$398.12*	*$90.00*	*$5.97*	*$84.03*	*$314.09*
Month 7	*$314.09*	*$90.00*	*$4.71*	*$85.29*	*$228.80*
Month 8	*$228.80*	*$90.00*	*$3.43*	*$86.57*	*$142.23*
Month 9	*$142.23*	*$90.00*	*$2.13*	*$87.87*	*$54.36*
Month 10	*$54.36*	*$55.18*	*$0.82*	*$54.36*	*$0.00*

Total Paid: $865.18   Interest Paid: $65.18

11. Explain that when people make credit card purchases, they receive a monthly credit card statement that contains information about their purchases, payments, and fees.

12. To show an example of a credit card statement, distribute copies of **Exercise 15.3** from the *Student Workbook*. Discuss the various components, making sure the students understand the following:

- Total credit line: The maximum amount that a cardholder can charge.

- Total available credit: Total credit line minus the new balance.

- Cash limit: Maximum amount that can be used for a cash advance.

- Cash available: Cash limit minus new balance.

- Amount past due: Any amount that was not paid on time.

- Statement closing date: The date when the credit card company calculates each period's new charges and computes new amounts that must be paid.

- New balance: The total amount of credit in use.

- Payment due date: Date by which the minimum payment must be made.

- Minimum payment: The least amount that must be paid to avoid a penalty.

- Previous balance: Last period's ending balance.

- Payments: How much was paid in the last billing period.

- Other credits: Any refunds posted to the account in the last billing period.

- Purchases: Total amount spent on new transactions in the billing cycle; the amount is itemized in another part of the statement.

- Cash advances: Amount charged to this account for cash received.

- Other fees: Late fees or other service charges.

- Finance charge: Interest incurred on previous balance.

- Grace period: Time when no interest is charged on new purchases if the new balance is paid in full by the payment due date.

13. Demonstrate how the new balance was computed.

Previous balance	$345.55
	- 200.00
	145.55
Plus Purchases	207.64
Plus late fee	29.00
Plus finance charge	5.30
New Balance	**$387.49**

14. Have the students complete **Exercise 15.3**, working independently.

Answers to Exercise 15.3

1. *February 10, 2010.*

2. *December 20, 2009.*

3. *Fee for late payment.*

4. *The total available credit is $2,612.*

5. *$207.64*

6. *$200.00*

7. *$3,000.00*

8. *$2,612.00*

9. *$5.30*

10. *Because he or she did not pay the balance in full last month.*

11. *Answers will vary. The consumer is paying off a major portion of his or her credit card debt, but has had difficulty in making the monthly payments on time ($29 late fee).*

LESSON 15

CLOSURE

Tell the students that the Credit CARD Act, which signed into law in 2009, has changed many of the features that have traditionally pertained to credit cards. For example, a credit card can no longer be issued to someone under the age of 21, unless they have an adult co-signer or can provide evidence of a means to repay credit. There are also new restrictions related to explanations of minimum payments, limits on fees, etc. However, make sure students understand that, even though it may be several years until they begin to use a credit card, it is very important for them to begin to use wise credit practices.

ASSESSMENT

Distribute a copy of **Lesson 15 Assessment** from the *Student Workbook* to each student. Ask the students, working in groups of three or four, to prepare a panel discussion on credit that covers the topics found in this assessment. When the groups are ready to present their work, use the rubric from **Visual 15.4** to evaluate the groups' panel discussions.

EXTENSION

Students can learn the tools to maintaining good credit by solving the mystery presented at the Bad Credit Hotel. htttp://www.controlyour-credit.gov/ (Guide students to use the "hints" in the upper right corner.)

Advantages and Disadvantages of Various Methods of Payment

Payment Options	Advantages	Disadvantages

How a Check Works

1. Chad writes a $50 check to pay for music CDs.
2. The shop owner sends Chad's check to her bank (A).
3. Bank A processes Chad's check and sends it to Chad's bank (B).
4. Bank B deducts $50 from Chad's checking account, and electronically notifies Bank A of the transaction.
5. Bank A electronically adds $50 to the shop owner's account.
6. Bank B sends Chad his cancelled check (or copy) for this record.

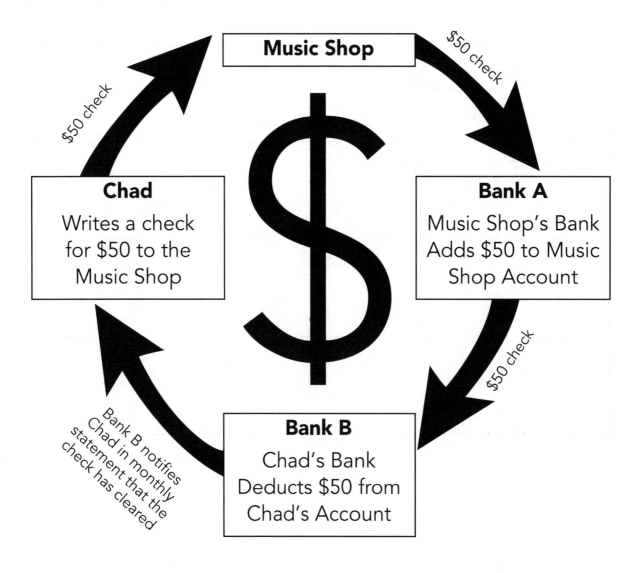

FINANCIAL FITNESS FOR LIFE: Teacher Guide Grades 6-8
http://fffl.councilforeconed.org/6-8

How a Credit Card Works

- Chad uses a credit card issued by ABC Credit Card Company to purchase video games.

- The store owner swipes Chad's credit card past a scanner.

- ABC Credit Card Company is quickly notified that Chad has requested $50 worth of credit , and if ABC Credit Card Company approves the charge, a credit sale occurs. The credit card company would add the amount of the item purchased to the store's bank account less a processing fee. The processing fee would go to the account of the store's merchant processor.

- ABC Credit Card Company sends Chad a statement that includes a record of his $50 purchase at the video store.

- If Chad has no balance on his credit card from the previous month, and pays the $50 before the due date, he usually won't have to pay any interest.

- If Chad chooses to pay only part of the $50, he will be charged interest on the remaining balance.

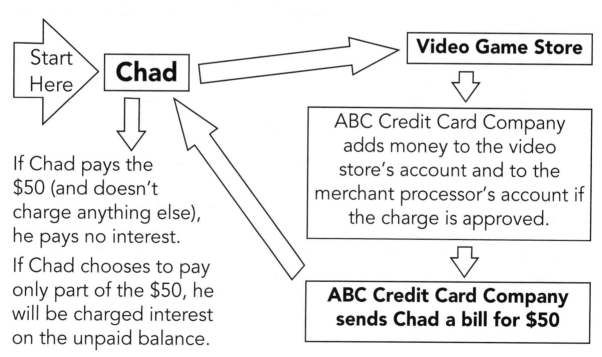

Lesson 15 Assessment: Answer Key

Rubric for Evaluating Panel Discussions

Topics to be covered in panel discussion	Discussed thoroughly and accurately 2 points	Briefly discussed with some inaccuracies 1 point	Not discussed 0 points
Advantages of using credit			
Disadvantages of using credit			
APR			
Grace Period			
Annual fees			
Transaction fees (late fees)			
Minimum payment and total cost			
Interesting statistics about credit			
Recommendations for wise credit use			
How inflation may affect decisions about use of credit			
The opportunity cost of credit			
Totals			
Grand Total of Three Columns			

FINANCIAL FITNESS FOR LIFE: Teacher Guide Grades 6-8
http://fffl.councilforeconed.org/6-8

Establishing Credit

LESSON DESCRIPTION AND BACKGROUND

Lenders are in business to grant loans to individuals and businesses. However, the applicant's ability to repay a loan can mean the difference between profit and loss for the lender. To reduce risk, the lender assesses the applicant's creditworthiness by reviewing his or her character, capacity for repayment and collateral. They also pay particular interest to the applicant's credit score. In this lesson, the students work through exercises to assess the three "Cs" of several loan applications. They discover how they can establish a credit record, and they learn about the rights and responsibilities they have as borrowers.

Lesson 16 is correlated with national standards for mathematics and economics, and with personal finance guidelines, as shown in Tables 1-3 in the introductory section of this publication.

ECONOMICS AND PERSONAL FINANCE CONCEPTS

- Credit history
- Credit score
- The three "Cs" of credit: character, capacity, collateral
- The rights and responsibilities of borrowers

OBJECTIVES

At the end of this lesson, the student will be able to:

- Identify and define the **three "Cs" of credit**.
- Explain how **credit history** is used to determine creditworthiness.
- Explain borrowers' rights when obtaining credit.
- Explain borrowers' responsibilities for managing credit.
- Describe ways in which a young person may establish credit.

TIME REQUIRED

Two 45-minute class periods

MATERIALS

- A copy for each student of **Introduction** and **Vocabulary** sections of **Lesson 16** from the *Student Workbook*
- A copy for each student of **Reading 16.1** from the *Student Workbook*
- Copies of **Exercise 16.1A**, **16.1B**, and **16.1C**, from the *Student Workbook* as specified in Procedure 3
- A copy for each student of **Exercise 16.1D** and **16.1E** from the *Student Workbook*
- A copy for each student of **Lesson 16 Assessment** from the *Student Workbook*

ADDITIONAL RESOURCES

To download visuals, find related lessons, correlations to state standards, interactives, and more, visit http://fffl.councilforeconed.org/6-8/lesson16.

PROCEDURE

1. Distribute a copy of **Introduction** and **Vocabulary** sections of **Lesson 16** in the *Student Workbook* to each student and use it to introduce the lesson's focus on credit. Sellers and credit-granting organizations, such as banks, provide consumers with credit. Credit is a loan extended to consumers or businesses.

2. Explain that those who provide credit are called "lenders." Lenders must use caution when granting credit, for an obvious reason; they do not want to lose money by making a bad loan. To guard against that risk, they look for certain characteristics among loan applicants. The characteristics are "character,"

"capacity," and "collateral." They are referred to in this lesson as "the three "Cs" of credit." Distribute copies of **Reading 16.1** from the *Student Workbook*; assign the students to do the reading. When they have finished the reading, review it with them to make sure they know what a lender looks for in evaluating the character, capacity, and collateral of a loan applicant.

3. Introduce the following activity as one in which the students will make use of the three "Cs" of credit as they examine loan applications.

a. Divide the class into six groups of students. Distribute copies of **Exercise 16.1A** to two groups, copies of **Exercise 16.1B** to two groups, and copies of **Exercise 16.1C** to two groups. Also give each student a copy of **Exercise 16.1E**.

b. Explain the task. In each group, the students should examine the loan application carefully, including the credit report. Then, based on information provided in the application, they should evaluate the applicant's creditworthiness by reference to the three "Cs" and recommend that the loan be granted or denied. They should use the Applicant Summary Sheet (**Exercise 16.1E**) to record their evaluations and recommendations.

c. Point out that the applications and credit reports shown in these exercises are not as lengthy as actual loan applications and credit reports. Still, the somewhat simplified exercise sheets will give the students enough information to make a decision. Help the students get started as necessary.

d. When each group has completed the task, a spokesperson from each group will present the group's assessment of the three Cs and the group's recommendation about the loan. Main points that should be addressed are noted below.

Answers to Exercise 16.1

Application 1: The Andersons

Character: *They pay their rent and make other payments on time.*

Capacity and Debt Ratios: *Required payments for credit before new loan are $332 ($180 + 90 + 62 = $332), which is 11.6 percent of their net monthly income, which is $2,863. With the new loan payment, required payments for credit would be $572 (19.98 percent of net income). This would put the Andersons just below the maximum amount they should be spending on consumer credit. The couple should be able to afford the new total of payments if there are no emergencies.*

Collateral: Acceptable. *They have $5,000 in cash (checking and savings).*

Recommendation: *Approve loan.*

Application 2: Joey Deligh

Character: *Has problems making required payments.*

Capacity and Debt Ratios: *Required payments for current debts are $1,338 (24 percent of his net monthly income). He should not take on any more debt. Even after paying off his old car, he will have 19 percent of his net income committed to debt ($500 + 348 + 125 + 75 = $1,048 ÷ 5,527 = 19 percent). If he drives his car for a while, he can save for a large down payment on another car sometime in the future. Assuming he doesn't sell his old car, if he were to buy a new car by borrowing $38,000, he would have 32.9 percent of his net income committed to debt ($500 + 348 + 125 + 75 + 773 = $1,821 ÷ 5,527 = 32.9 percent).*

Collateral: *Cash plus investments and equity in home is less than outstanding debt.*

Recommendation: *Would not approve loan.*

Application 3: The Ransdias

Character: *Good record of paying debts.*

Capacity: *Required payments for outstanding credit are $1,272 per month. Net monthly income is $10,028. Have sufficient earnings to pay bills. Even with the new*

loan, only 16.1 percent of income would be committed to consumer debt ($340 + 145 + 247 + 293 + 587 = $1,612 ÷ $10,028 = 16.1 percent).

Collateral: **Have more in collateral than loans.**

Recommendation: **Approve loan.**

4. Look back on **Exercise 16.1**, focusing on the fact that one of the applicants probably would not be approved for the loan he requested. From this observation, move on to introduce the concept of borrowers' rights and responsibilities.

a. Ask the students what they would do if they were denied a loan. **(The students may say that they would just do without the item they wished to purchase with the loan, that they would seek another source for a loan, or that they would seek information as to why they were denied the loan and take action to repair their credit reports. All of these answers are acceptable.)**

b. Explain that borrowers have "rights" and "responsibilities" associated with the credit they obtain. Each person has a right to view his or her credit report, for no charge, once a year. When an application for credit is denied, the applicant also has a right to view his or her credit report, for no charge, within 30 days of the denial. If any important information on the report is in error, the credit-reporting agency must change the information and notify lenders about the correction. If the applicant disagrees with the credit-reporting agency about information on the report, the applicant has a right to attach his or her explanation of the problem to the credit report. This explanation must also be sent to lenders. These rights for credit consumers are guaranteed by a law called the Fair Credit Reporting Act. It should also be noted that the Credit Card Accountability Responsibility and Disclosure Act of 2009 (or Credit CARD Act of 2009) contains provisions that, among other things, includes a Credit Cardholders' Bill of Rights.

c. Explain that borrowers also have other rights, including the following:

- The right to information about the Annual Percentage Rate (APR) and the total finance charges for a loan in question.

- Eligibility for credit without discrimination based on gender, religion, race, nationality, or marital status.

- The right to contest charges on your credit card statement if you think they are wrong.

- Protection from abuse by credit collection agencies if you are late making payments.

5. Explain that along with these rights come responsibilities. Ask the students what some responsibilities may be. **(Borrowers are responsible for repayment of the loan plus interest, making payments on time, providing accurate information on credit applications.)**

6. Shift the emphasis to a consideration of the students' own creditworthiness.

a. Ask: Would it be easy or difficult for you to get approved for a loan today? **(Difficult, because students [as a rule] have no income, collateral, or credit history.)**

b. With the students, turn back to the first page of **Reading 16.1**. Use the section on young people seeking to borrow money as the basis for a discussion of how the students might begin soon to establish and develop a good credit history. **(Possibilities include open a checking or savings account [and don't bounce a check], obtain a department store credit card by getting an adult to be a co-signer on the credit application [and make your payments in full and on time], etc.)**

CLOSURE

Use the following questions to review the lesson.

- When a lender is considering your "character", what does he or she examine? **(Your record of paying your debts on** time; your history of managing finances, such as a checking account; your employment stability; and your residential stability.)

- When a lender is considering your "capacity," what characteristics does he or she examine? **(Your income from all sources; your assets; your current debts; and your net worth [the difference between everything you own and everything you owe to others].)**

- Lenders want to be sure you won't just walk away from a loan without paying. They want to be sure you have "collateral." What types of things might serve as collateral for a loan? **(A car, a house, etc.)**

- If you have no credit history, what might you do to establish credit? **(Open a checking or savings account, establish a department store account or a layaway plan, obtain a small starter loan or credit card, get a co-signer for a loan.)**

- What rights do you have as a borrower? **(You are eligible to be considered for a loan without discrimination based on gender, race, religion, nationality, or marital status; you must be provided with information about interest rates and fees; you cannot be subject to abusive credit collection practices; you can obtain a free copy of your credit report once a year from each of the credit reporting agencies.)**

- What are your responsibilities as a borrower? **(You must make at least the minimum payment when payment is due; you must pay any applicable finance charge; you must pay late fees for late payments.)**

ASSESSMENT

Distribute a copy of **Exercise 16.1D** and **Lesson 16 Assessment** from the *Student Workbook* to each student. Assign the students to complete the assessment, working independently. The task is to evaluate the loan application for Rhett Willis, shown on **Exercise 16.1D**.

Answers to Lesson 16 Assessment

Character: Sometimes has difficulty making payments on time, especially in the last six months. Always makes payments, though. Capacity: Savings and checking account balances are more than credit card debt. Required payments for outstanding debts are $305, 9.6 percent of his net monthly income of $3,174. After the new loan, his payments will be $544 (17.1 percent of his net monthly income—more than is recommended, but less than the maximum of 20 percent of net monthly income that should be committed to debt.) Collateral: Motor home counts as collateral. Would recommend that the loan be granted.)

EXTENSION

Instruct students to create a "Note to Self." Explain that in just a few years, they will be interested in using credit, in the form of credit cards, a car loan, or student loans. Their character, capacity, and collateral will determine whether they are extended credit, how much credit they are offered, and the interest rate they will be obligated to pay.

Remind students of their examination of credit applications. Which would they have denied and which would they have accepted? What details in the applicant's credit histories reflected poorly on the applicant?

In their note, students should instruct themselves on how they will prove themselves to be creditworthy by addressing character, capacity and collateral. For example, a student could show good character by managing his or her checking account responsibly or by paying a cell phone bill on time. He or she could show capacity by getting a part-time job. Collateral could include money saved in a saving account.

Comparison Shopping

LESSON DESCRIPTION AND BACKGROUND

The students identify costs and benefits of comparison shopping. They learn about a seven-step approach that can help consumers make well-informed choices, and they practice using it. They also learn to avoid certain mistakes that consumers often make.

For some people, shopping is an art, and they spend hours and hours making a decision about what to buy. For others, the goal is to get in, buy it, and get out! Neither of these approaches is necessarily efficient. Making good choices requires a plan of action—one that doesn't take too much of the consumer's time and doesn't place the consumer in a vulnerable position, misinformed or intimidated.

Lesson 17 is correlated with national standards for mathematics and economics, and with personal finance guidelines, as shown in Tables 1-3 in the introductory section of this publication.

ECONOMIC AND PERSONAL FINANCE CONCEPTS

- Comparison shopping
- Consumer protection

OBJECTIVES

At the end of this lesson, the student will be able to:

- State the seven steps consumers can use in deciding what to buy.
- Explain why each step of a consumer decision-making process is important.
- Use a seven-step process in making a decision.
- Describe illegal or deceptive practices found in the marketplace.
- Identify the advantages and disadvantages of **comparison shopping**.
- Identify not-for-profit or government agencies

that provide services for consumers.

TIME REQUIRED

Two or three 45-minute class periods

MATERIALS

- A transparency of **Visual 17.1** and **17.2**

- A copy for each student of **Introduction** and **Vocabulary** sections of **Lesson 17** from the *Student Workbook*

- A copy for each student of **Exercise 17.1**, **17.2**, **17.3**, and **17.4** from the *Student Workbook*

- A copy for each student of **Reading 17.1** and **17.2** from the *Student Workbook*

- A copy for each student of **Lesson 17 Assessment** from the *Student Workbook*

- Store advertisements, newspaper ads, and online ads for the following consumer products: home theater system, laptop computer, used car, flat-screen TV, refrigerator. (The teacher may substitute other consumer products.)

ADDITIONAL RESOURCES

To download visuals, find related lessons, correlations to state standards, interactives, and more, visit http://fffl.councilforeconed.org/6-8/lesson17.

PROCEDURE

1. Introduce the lesson by explaining that people often make financial mistakes through haste and unreliable information, or no information at all. This applies especially to decisions people make about what to buy. Assign the students to read the Introduction and Vocabulary sections

for **Lesson 17** from the *Student Workbook*. Distribute copies of **Exercise 17.1** from the *Student Workbook*. Read the two adages aloud. Be sure to explain that "pound" in this case refers to the United Kingdom pound sterling (the UK currency) and not a pound in weight. Then ask the students what they think the two adages mean. Discuss their responses briefly.

2. Provide additional clarification of the two adages, as necessary. The first one refers to people who make an effort to save a penny, but do so in ways that cost them much more than a penny later on. For example, somebody buys a low-quality product because it is cheap—and then it falls apart. Or somebody is very careful in making small purchases but careless with large purchases. The second adage suggests that people should be careful with even their smallest purchases, because any amount of money saved is like receiving that amount in income. Together, the adages suggest that it is best to be careful with all purchases, large and small.

3. Bring up another adage: that "People should try to live within their means." Ask the students what this adage means. Discuss their responses briefly; then, as necessary, explain the adage as a recommendation that people should limit their expenditures to their amount of income. Suggest that this is good advice—though it might be even better if people would live "beneath" their means. Ask: What might that mean, and why might it be better? *(The students might suggest, for example, that although someone could afford to buy a car requiring a payment of $400 per month, that person might be better off finding a car she could buy for $350 per month. Then she would have $50 extra each month to apply to savings.)*

4. Advise the students that living beneath your means would not necessarily mean doing without the things you want. By managing your money well, you may be able to stay within your budget, or spend even less than your budget allows. In your efforts to do this, one important practice is comparison shopping.

5. Explain the term "comparison shopping." Basically, it refers to looking around for a while, making comparisons, before buying something. For example, a comparison shopper shopping for blue jeans might check out different brands and models, and the same brands and models at different stores, in order to find the best fit, the most attractive style, and the best price. Ask:

a. Do you do comparison shopping for the things you buy? *(Answers will vary.)*

b. Why might a person not do comparison shopping, or not do it all the time? *(Answers will vary. Comparison shopping may seem to be too time-consuming; people sometimes know exactly what they want and where to buy it; etc.)*

6. Distribute copies of **Reading 17.1** from the *Student Workbook*. Have the students do the reading. Discuss the advantages and disadvantages of comparison shopping. Write the following statement on the board:

"Comparison shopping is more important for expensive, complex products than for inexpensive, simple products."

Ask: How does this statement relate to the advantages and disadvantages we have discussed? Are the advantages and disadvantages the same when we are talking about shopping for expensive, complex products? *(Comparison shopping may well be more important in buying a computer than, say, in buying a celebrity magazine or a package of chewing gum. In the case of the computer, the costs of a bad decision might be great; in the other cases, differences among products and prices might be small, so that weighing them might not be worth a great deal of the shopper's time.)*

7. Remind the students of the concept of "opportunity cost." It refers to the next-best alternative a person gives up in making a decision. Ask: How does the concept of opportunity cost relate to decisions about comparison shopping? *(The opportunity cost of*

comparison shopping is the time, and sometimes the money, comparison shopping takes. This time and money could be used in other ways. Comparison shopping for simple, inexpensive things, therefore, may not seem worthwhile. Generally, however, the benefits shoppers gain from careful shopping are worth more than the time and money given up.)

8. Explain that the students soon will have an opportunity to demonstrate their ability to get value for their money. However, they must first learn a strategy to use in comparison shopping. Display **Visual 17.1**. Discuss the steps as follows.

- **Identify what you want.** This may seem obvious, but writing down exactly what you want helps you avoid the impulse to buy things on the spur of the moment or to buy something that is low on your list of priorities.

- **Determine how much you can spend or want to spend.** You know how much money you have budgeted for purchases. Determine how much you can spend, within your budget, and stick to your decision. It's very easy to rationalize spending only a few dollars more than you intended to. However, if you do this with every item you purchase, you will eventually have to do without something you want when your money runs out.

- **Find out what products or services are available in your price range.** Determine the price range you can afford, and look at the options in that price range. Don't look at more expensive options that are out of your price range; they may tempt you to buy an item you cannot afford.

- **Choose the features you would most like to have.** List the features that are important to you—size, color, style, materials, etc.—so that you can compare the products in your price range by reference to these features.

- **Use the decision-making grid to analyze the alternatives.** This will help you analyze the products in your price range that have the features you desire. Display **Visual 17.2**, which shows a completed decision-making grid for someone considering the purchase of a DVD player. Follow these steps in using the grid:

  a. List the alternatives along the side of the left-most column—in this case, the various brands of the DVD player.

  b. List the features that you want along the top of the grid. These include universal remote, high definition, Blu-ray media, MPEG compatible, Dolby sound.

  c. If a product you are considering has the feature, place a plus sign (+) in the appropriate cell. If the product does not have the feature, place a minus sign (-) in the appropriate cell.

  d. Tally the plusses for the respective products to determine which one would be the best choice, according to this analysis.

- **Watch for hidden costs.** Before making a final choice, look for any hidden costs associated with the alternatives you are considering, especially the alternative that is most attractive to you. These costs might include delivery costs, special taxes or surcharges, required accessories, or club membership. High hidden costs may encourage you to select a product other than your first choice.

- **Make your choice.** Decide on what you want, and stick to your decision. After using the good or service, determine whether it was a wise choice.

9. Arrange for the students to practice comparison shopping. Divide the class into groups of three or four.

- Assign each team one of the products below. Have the students choose the store, newspaper, or online ads featuring their consumer item. Use suggested budget limits or any reasonable budget limits for stores in your area.

  Home theater system ($1,500 budget)

  Laptop computer ($800 budget)

Used car ($5,000 budget)

Flat screen TV ($800 budget)

Refrigerator ($900 budget)

- Distribute copies of **Exercise 17.2** from the *Student Workbook*, which includes a decision-making grid for the students to use in analyzing the various options and making a decision.

- To gather information about the product that they have been assigned, the students may read the advertising that you have supplied and/or do comparison shopping on the Internet or in the local community.

- When the students have completed their decision-making activity, have them present their choices and explain how they arrived at their choices to the class.

10. Turn to the topic of hindrances to good decision making. Explain that even carefully-made decisions sometimes fail to satisfy consumers. This happens for various reasons. Sometimes the consumer has not been well informed. Sometimes the consumer will have felt pressured into making a decision against his or her better judgment.

11. Distribute copies of **Exercise 17.3** from the *Student Workbook*. Choose three students to perform the play, *Poor Mrs. Amos*. Tell the class to follow along as the play is performed, paying particular attention to the tactics used by the salesman. When the students have performed the play, discuss the questions found at the end the exercise.

Answers to Exercise 17.3

1. The salesman intimidated Mrs. Amos by comparing her yard to her neighbors' yards. He told her many of her peers use the lawn service. He trivialized the cost of the service.

2. If Mrs. Amos was uncomfortable with his tactics, she should have hung up the phone.

3. Mrs. Amos continued to stay on the phone because she was polite; she did not want to appear rude; she was trusting.

12. Explain that the cost of lawn service may be relatively small, but the items offered by telephone sales people are often costly. Many people have been "talked out of" very large amounts of money to buy everything from land to securities to insurance policies. This practice isn't limited to telephone sales, however. Consumers can walk into a sales office to buy cars, large appliances, or vacation homes and become just as intimidated.

13. Turn to a different example. Distribute copies of **Exercise 17.4** from the *Student Workbook*. Choose four students to perform the play, *The Worm Has Turned*. The four students will play Mr. Allen, Tina Allen, the salesman, and the sales manager. The sales manager has no speaking part. Place the salesman, Mr. Allen, and Tina Allen around a desk. Place the sales manager in a corner of the room. Quietly instruct the sales manager and the salesman to pantomime an argument in the corner when the script calls for the salesman to meet with the sales manager.

14. When the play has been performed, discuss the questions from the exercise sheet.

Answers to Exercise 17.4

1. The salesman tried to be very friendly with Tina and her father by asking Tina if she had just received her license; he discussed his own teenagers; he kept telling Tina and her father how much he liked them; he told them he would go to the manager on their behalf.

2. The salesman tried to pressure Tina and her father by indicating that there was another customer coming in to buy the car.

3. Answers will vary, but the students will probably think Tina was going to succumb to the pressure.

4. Tina did the right thing. She and her dad had a budgeted amount for the car they would buy, and they stuck to their budget.

15. Warn the students about other types of consumer pitfalls they should avoid. Distribute copies of **Reading 17.2** and have the students do the reading. Engage them in a discussion of examples of these practices that they may have observed. Share your own observations about such practices.

16. Explain that various federal, state, and local laws have been enacted to protect consumers against fraud and other illegal sales practices. There are also not-for-profit organizations consumers can consult before buying a product or when they are having problems with a product already purchased. Tell the students that they can find websites for consumers by searching online for "consumer protection."

17. In addition, the students can protect themselves in the following ways:

- Ask friends about their experiences with a given store or sales office.

- Before making a purchase, consult the Better Business Bureau (BBB). You can call or visit it online at http://www.bbb.org. The BBB keeps lists of consumer complaints against stores and sales offices. The BBB works with consumers and stores or sales offices to deal with complaints. The BBB can offer you information BEFORE you buy.

- Your state's Attorney General's office accepts consumer complaints. It will work with the consumer and the store or sales office to deal with complaints. It may also prosecute stores and sales offices if illegal practices are suspected.

- The Federal Trade Commission (FTC, at http://www.ftc.gov) acts by authority of federal laws to protect consumers.

- The National Consumer League maintains a website for reporting incidents of telephone and Internet fraud. This site is located at http://www.fraud.org.

CLOSURE

Use the following questions to review the lesson.

- The first step in a decision about a purchase is to identify what you want. Why is this step so important? *(It forces you to define exactly what you want. By defining your wants, you avoid impulse buying.)*

- The second step is to determine how much you can spend. Why is this step so important? *(By setting a firm budget for the item, you can avoid being lured into spending more than you want to spend.)*

- The third step is to find out what products or services are available in your price range. Why is this step so important? *(In order to be a well-informed consumer and get exactly what you want, you have to seek out options that are available to you.)*

- The fourth step is to choose the features you would like to have. Why is this step so important? *(This helps you to make comparisons among products, and it increases the likelihood that you will be happy with your decision.)*

- The fifth step is to analyze the alternatives according to the features that you want, using a decision-making grid. Why is it important to analyze the alternatives? *(To determine which choice is best for you, according to the features you have specified.)*

- The sixth step is to watch for hidden costs. Why is this step so important? *(You don't want the final cost of your purchase to exceed your budget.)*

- What is the seventh step? *(It is to make your choice.)*

- How would you describe "bait and switch" selling? *(This is an illegal practice where the consumer is lured into a store to purchase a bargain-priced product only to be told the product is "sold out," and then steered toward a pricier item.)*

- Can you give any examples of deceptive pricing? *(Many possible answers—e.g., stores may offer a "special value," hoping to persuade the consumer that something is on sale at a reduced price when it actually is not.)*

- Can you give any examples of deceptive advertising? *(Many possible answers— e.g., an advertisement may fail to disclose the fact that a bargain is available only when a related product is purchased at its normal price.)*

- If you are considering a purchase, how can you know you are dealing with a reputable store or sales office? *(Ask other people about their experiences with the store or sales office. Consult the Better Business Bureau or other consumer-advocacy organizations in your community.)*

ASSESSMENT

Distribute copies of **Lesson 17 Assessment**. Assign the students to complete the assessment, working independently. Tell them to choose a small item (under $75) they would like to purchase and follow the procedures they learned in this lesson. Answers will vary according to the good or service selected and the criteria (features) used to evaluate the alternatives.

EXTENSION

It is a good idea to check with the Better Business Bureau when contemplating a repair, a remodel, or a major purchase of any kind. Place the students in small groups and have them visit the Better Business Bureau website at http://www.bbb.org. Instruct them to find the office nearest them by using their zip code or by using the directory. Instruct them to click on the "Type of Business" tab. Enter a business type such as payday loans or auto repair. Have the students choose a business and take notes on the type of information that is provided. Challenge the students to find a business with complaints. Have them report on the type of

complaints the Better Business Bureau has received and whether the complaints were resolved.

Major Steps in Deciding What to Buy

1. Identify what you want.

- Set your priorities. • Avoid impulse buying.

2. Determine how much you can spend or want to spend.

- Develop a budget and stick to it.

3. Find out what products or services are available in your price range.

- Check store ads.   • Consult consumer magazines.
- Ask your friends.   • Visit online vendors.

4. Choose the features you would most like to have.

- List specific characteristics/features the goods/services must have and features that it would be nice to have (optional).
- List the characteristics/features you definitely do not want.

5. Use the decision-making grid to analyze the alternatives.

- Use **+** for alternatives that have a desired feature,
  – for alternatives without the feature.
- Tally the plusses to determine best choice.

6. Watch for hidden costs.

- Check the sales tax. (Sales tax varies by community.)
- Check for delivery costs or costs of required accessories.

7. Make your choice.

Decision-making Grid for a DVD Player

Features ➡️ ⬇️ Alternatives	Feature 1 Universal Remote	Feature 2 high definition	Feature 3 Blu-ray Media	Feature 4 MPEG compatible	Feature 5 Dolby Sound	Total Points
Item 1	+	–	–	+	+	3
Item 2	+	–	–	–	+	2
Item 3	+	–	+	–	–	2
Item 4	+	+	+	+	–	4

FINANCIAL FITNESS FOR LIFE: Teacher Guide Grades 6-8
http://fffl.councilforeconed.org/6-8

Notes:

Notes:

Notes:

_____

_____

_____

_____

_____

_____

_____

_____

_____

_____

_____

_____

_____

_____

_____

_____

_____

_____

_____

_____

_____

Notes:

_____

_____

_____

_____

_____

_____

_____

_____

_____

_____

_____

_____

_____

_____

_____

_____

_____

_____

_____

_____

_____

FINANCIAL FITNESS FOR LIFE: Teacher Guide Grades 6-8
http://fffl.councilforeconed.org/6-8